Company Erie Railroad

Homes and Sports along the Erie

A Directory to Hotels, Boarding Houses, Lakes and Streams...

Company Erie Railroad

Homes and Sports along the Erie
A Directory to Hotels, Boarding Houses, Lakes and Streams...

ISBN/EAN: 9783337020521

Printed in Europe, USA, Canada, Australia, Japan

Cover: Foto ©Andreas Hilbeck / pixelio.de

More available books at **www.hansebooks.com**

SUMMER SPORTS
HOMES AND
Along the ERIE

1881

PRESENTED BY THE PASSENGER DEPARTMENT OF THE NEW YORK LAKE ERIE & WESTERN RAILROAD.

JNO. N. ABBOTT,
Gen'l Pass'r Ag't,
NEW YORK.

E. S. BOWEN,
Gen'l Sup't,
NEW YORK.

ANTI-MALARIAL RESORTS.

In presenting this GUIDE to the public the Erie Railway Company has kept in view the fact that people seeking sojourning places in the country especially desire to avoid all localities subject to malarial influences. The Erie is peculiarly fortunate in the anti-malarial character of the country through which it passes. The pure air, rapid waters, and high elevations of the Ramapo, Delaware, and Neversink valleys, and the back regions of Ulster, Sullivan, Orange, Pike, Wayne, and Delaware counties, are persistent foes to the diseases that have become so prevalent in other parts of the country. Malaria cannot originate in the above localities, and physicians are annually sending patients afflicted with malarial affections to the above health-renewing resorts along the Erie.

COMMUTATION TICKETS MAY BE OBTAINED AT THE COMPANY'S OFFICE, 187 WEST STREET.

A TOPOGRAPHICAL MAP,

Showing the Lakes, Streams, Mountains, and all points of interest mentioned in this book will be issued by the Erie Railway Company in June of this year. Copies of the map, as well as time-tables, circulars, &c., may be had on application at the offices of the Company, 261, 401, 957 Broadway, N. Y.; 2 Court street, Brooklyn; 34 Hudson street, Hoboken; 184 Market street, Newark; at station ticket offices along the line, or by mail to

JOHN N. ABBOTT,
General Passenger Agent,
N. Y.

HOMES AND SPORTS
ALONG THE ERIE.

A DIRECTORY

TO

Hotels, Boarding Houses,

LAKES AND STREAMS,

IN THE

ROMANTIC REGIONS NEAR NEW YORK,

REACHED BY THE

ERIE RAILWAY.

ISSUED BY THE GENERAL PASSENGER DEPARTMENT
OF THE COMPANY

NEW YORK:
MARTIN B. BROWN, PRINTER, 49 AND 51 PARK PLACE.
1881.

TO

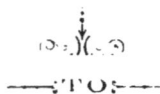

HAY-FEVER AND ASTHMATIC

SUFFERERS.

IN THE

MOUNTAIN REGIONS

OF

NEW YORK and PENNSYLVANIA,

REACHED BY THE

Erie Railway,

YOU WILL FIND

RELIEF IN A SHORT TIME.

As a Sanitarium for these complaints they are UNSURPASSED by the climate of the White Mountains, as hundreds can and do testify.

All trains on the Erie Railway leave New York from the foot of Chambers and 23d Sts., North River.

ALONG THE EASTERN DIVISION.

RUTHERFURD, PASSAIC CO., N. J.

9 Miles from New York : 15 Trains each way daily
5 from and 3 to New York Sunday.

FARE—LOCAL, 30 CENTS. EXCURSION, 40 CENTS. COMMUTATION
3 MOS., $19.

A place of suburban homes. Pure water in abundance. Methodist,
Episcopal, Baptist and Presbyterian churches. Fine fishing and boating in the Passaic river. Splendid drives, walks and shady groves.

BOARDING HOUSES.

"LYNDHURST"—EDGAR A. ROBERTS, Proprietor—1¼ mile from
depot. Transportation 25 cents. Accommodations for 30 ; 6 single
rooms ; 12 double rooms ; $7.50 single ; $10 to $12 double ; $1.50 per
day. Discount to season guests. Farm attached. Raises vegetables.
On Passaic river. Recommended to amateur oarsmen and athletes.
Provides boats for fishermen at $1 per day ; lower for season.

MRS. VAN RIPER—Five minutes from depot. Accommodations for
10 ; 2 single rooms ; 4 double rooms ; $6 single ; $12 double. Raises
vegetables.

PASSAIC BRIDGE.

11 Miles from New York : 11 Trains from and 14
Trains to New York daily ; 3 Trains each way
Sunday.

HOTEL.

PARK HOTEL—Near depot ; accommodations for 150 ; desirable
double rooms and suites for families ; $9 to $25. Elegantly furnished.
Large park.

BOARDING HOUSE.

JOHN S. CONKLING—½ mile from depot at *Passaic Bridge*. Free
transportation. Accommodations for 12 ; 3 single rooms ; 5 double
rooms—$8 to $10 single ; $10 to $12 for double. Discount to season
guests. Raises vegetables.

PASSAIC, PASSAIC COUNTY, N. J.

12 Miles from New York: 15 Trains from and 17 to
New York daily; 6 Trains from and 4 to
New York Sunday.

FARE—LOCAL, 10 CENTS. EXCURSION, 55 CENTS. COMMUTATION,
3 MOS., $21.

A beautiful city. Residence of many New York business men.
Well governed. Churches of several denominations. Best schools.
Dundee Lake three miles distant—reached by charming drive.
Famous mineral spring on Paulison Heights. Elevated points of
interest. In the heart of the Passaic valley. Residents cultured and
refined Fine boating and fishing in the Passaic river. P. O. address
for Passaic Bridge.

———✗✗———

BOARDING HOUSES.

THE ANDERSON MANSION—MRS. R. B. TOWNER, Proprietor—
Five minutes walk from depot at Prospect street. On banks of
Passaic. Accommodations for 30: 2 single rooms; 14 double rooms—
$7 per week for single room: $12 to $16 for double room. Transient,
$1 per day. Discount to season guests. Raises vegetables. Plenty of
fresh milk and eggs. Farm of forty acres attached. Shaded lawn of
three acres. Large halls, closets, piazzas.

MRS. CANFIELD—Opposite the depot. Accommodations for 15:
$6 to $12.

MRS. HARDWICK—On the Heights. Short walk from the depot.
Accommodations for 15 : $6 to $12.

LIVERY.

J. T. VAN ORDEN, J. A. SPROULL, H. W. SANDERS—$3 to $5
per day, single rig; team, $6 to $10.

———◆○◎◆●◆———

CLIFTON, PASSAIC COUNTY, N. J.

13½ Miles from New York: 11 Trains from and 15
to New York daily; 8 Trains from and 8
to New York Sunday.

FARE—LOCAL, 45c.; EXCURSION, 65c.; COMMUTATION, 3 mos., $21.50.

A charming rural spot. Fine drives to Paterson, Passaic, Rutherford,
Hackensack and Belleville. Dundee Lake, a popular resort for boating
and fishing, within a short walk.

———✗✗———

HOTEL.

CLIFTON GROVE HOUSE J. B. GREIBEL, Proprietor—Three
minutes walk from depot. Accommodations for 40: $7 to $10. Rooms
large and airy. Piazzas and grounds. Large pic-nic grove attached.
Good water. Surroundings healthful.

2

LAKE VIEW, PASSAIC COUNTY, N. J.

15 Miles from New York : 11 Trains from and 14 Trains to New York daily ; 3 Trains from and 3 Trains to New York Sunday.

FARE—LOCAL, 50c.; EXCURSION, 70c.; COMMUTATION, 3 mos., $22.

A quiet and attractive suburb of Paterson, on high ground, and over-looking the Passaic Valley, at Dundee Lake, a few minutes walk from the depot. Fine boating and fishing in the Passaic. A most convenient and pleasing spot to spend the summer months. Th' village site, east of the railroad, is on the brow of a ridge sloping gradually in one direction, and abruptly in the other, making the drainage perfect.

— ❄ —

HOTEL.

LAKE VIEW HOTEL—P. H. MACE, Proprietor—Three minutes walk from depot. Accommodations for 20 : $8 to $10 ; $2.50 per day. 1 mile from Passaic river. Boating and fishing. Livery attached, $4 per day.

◄ ◆ ● ◆ ►

PATERSON, PASSAIC CO., N. J.

17 Miles from New York : 27 Trains from New York and 32 Trains to New York daily ; 8 Trains from New York and 10 to New York Sunday.

Paterson is a city of 50,000 inhabitants, and is a place of great manu-factories. While not strictly a resort for summer guests, its fine sur-roundings attract many visitors. Passaic Falls, one of the famous cataracts of this country, is in the heart of the city. The United States Hotel is a first class and conveniently located hostelry.

◄ ◆ ● ◆ ►

HAWTHORNE, PASSAIC COUNTY, N. J.

19 Miles from New York : 6 Trains from and 7 Trains to New York daily ; 4 Trains from and 3 to New York Sunday.

FARE—LOCAL, 60c.; EXCURSION, 85c.; COMMUTATION, 3 mos., $23.50.

On the outskirts of Paterson, across the Passaic. Preakness Hills on the west. Farming neighborhood. Elevated ground. Good fishing in the Passaic. Fine drives. Livery at Paterson. Passaic Falls, 1 mile.

— ❄ —

BOARDING HOUSES.

C. J. ACKERMAN—½ mile from depot. Transportation 25 cents. Accommodations for 10 : 4 single rooms ; 3 double rooms—$6. No dis-count. Furnishes boat. Raises vegetables.

MRS. JAMES FENNER -¾ mile from depot. Conveyance. Accom-modations for 8— $6 to $8 ; children half price.

P. D. WESTERVELT—¾ mile from depot. Conveyance. Accom-modations for 4—$6 to $8.

RIDGEWOOD, BERGEN COUNTY, N. J.

22 Miles from New York : 8 Trains from and 7 to
New York daily ; 4 Trains from and 8 to
New York Sunday.

FARE— LOCAL, 70c.; EXCURSION, 95c., COMMUTATION, 3 mos., $25.00.

In the heart of the Paramus Valley. Pastoral region. Residence of
celebrated public men. Much of antiquarian interest in the neighborhood. Best of drives.

—:—

FARM HOUSE.

GEORGE J. HOPPER 2¼ miles from depot. Accommodations for
8 - $6. 1½ miles from Passaic river. Plenty of shade. Vegetables and
fruit in abundance.

◄►◄►

HOHOKUS, BERGEN COUNTY, N. J.

24 Miles from New York : 7 Trains from and 8 to
New York daily ; 4 Trains from and 8 to
New York Sunday.

FARE—LOCAL, 75c.; EXCURSION, $1 ; COMMUTATION, 3 mos., $26.00.

A picturesque and interesting spot in the Paramus Valley. Revolutionary ground. Residence of Joseph Jefferson, the celebrated actor.
Ancient church, turned into a prison for American prisoners by the
British, still standing. Home of Theodosia Prevost when Aaron Burr
paid his court to her. Fine drives and walks.

—:—

BOARDING HOUSES.

J. A. OSBORNE—½ mile from depot. Free transportation to and
from two trains, morning and evening. For irregular trains, 25 cents.
Accommodations for 15 : 3 single rooms ; 6 double rooms—$10 per
week for single room ; $16 per week for double ; transient $1.50 per day.
Vegetables from the farm.

JOHN J. VOORHEES—¾ mile from depot. Free transportation.
Accommodations for 12 : 6 single rooms—$7—$1.50 per day. Raises
vegetables.

J. N. LEMON—1½ miles from depot. Free carriage. Accommodations for 20 : 2 single rooms ; 7 double rooms —$7 to $8. Discount to
season guests. On Saddle river ; boats free ; 60 acres. Spring water.
Plenty shade. Good drives. Vegetables, fruit, eggs, Alderney milk,
butter, chickens, from the farm.

J. A. ZABRISKIE 1 mile from depot. Free carriage. Accommodations for 15 : 2 single rooms ; 2 double rooms. Will give rates to appli-
cants. Raises vegetables. Fishing and boating near. Furnishes
livery.

BROOKSIDE FARM –H. C. DENNETT, Proprietor—1½ miles from
depot. Guests going to and coming from city on business transported
free ; pleasure, 25 cents. Accommodations for 30 : 5 single rooms ; 8
double rooms—$6.50 single ; $8 and $8.50 double ; $1.25 per day. From
Saturday night till Monday morning, $3. Nurse girls not taken. Stream
for boating on the premises. Boats free. Pure drinking water. Fresh
vegetables, fruit, milk, eggs, and butter from the farm—100 acres.

4

ALLENDALE, BERGEN CO., N. J.

26 Miles from New York: 8 Trains each way daily;
5 Trains from and 3 to New York Sunday.

FARE LOCAL, 80c.; EXCURSION, $1 10; COMMUTATION, 3 MONTHS, $28.

A breezy hamlet among farms and hills and orchards. Great fruit-growing region. Pure water and air.

—❊—

BOARDING HOUSE.

W. A. ACKERMAN—Two miles from depot. Free transportation. Accommodations for 16; 8 double rooms; $7 per week. Transient, $2 over Sunday. Discount to season guests. Raises vegetables. High ground. No malaria or mosquitos.

—◆●◆●— —

RAMSEY'S, BERGEN CO., N. J.

28 Miles from New York: 8 Trains each way daily;
5 Trains from and 3 to New York Sunday.

FARE—LOCAL, 85c.; EXCURSION, $1.15; COMMUTATION, 3 MONTHS, $29.

High ground. Outlet of Ramapo Valley. Darlington, the famous stock farm of A. B. Darling, of the Fifth Avenue Hotel, is near. Trout streams in the mountains, easy of access. Points of interest connected with the Revolution. Healthful. Splendid drives. Great fruit growing region.

—❊—

HOTEL.

FOWLER HOUSE—Near depot. Attention to sportsmen. Livery attached. Guide furnished.

BOARDING HOUSES.

A. DE BAUN—2½ miles from depot. Transportation free. Accommodations for 20; 9 rooms; $6 to $8. On Saddle River. Raises vegetables and fruits.

SHADY LAWN HOUSE—A. H. ACKERMAN, Proprietor—1 mile from depot. Transportation free. Accommodations for 25; 2 single rooms; 10 double rooms. Terms moderate. Broad piazzas. Extensive lawn. Horses and carriages furnished. Mountain scenery. Plenty of shade. Large airy rooms. Fresh vegetables, fruit, milk, butter and eggs on farm. Plenty of ice.

MRS. D. VALENTINE—Near depot. Accommodations for 10. Large airy rooms. Terms moderate.

MRS. J. W. VALENTINE—Near depot. Accommodations for 10. Large airy rooms. Terms moderate.

REV. E. DEYO—Ten minutes walk from depot. Accommodations for 10. Reasonable terms. High ground.

5

L. VON NIEZINESKY—1 miles from depot. Accommodations
for 25. House thoroughly repaired for season. Generally patronized
by Germans.

FARM HOUSE.

ISAAC RAMSEY—1¼ miles from depot. Accommodations for 10.
Terms moderate.

A. A. ACKERMAN—1¼ mile from depot. Accommodations for 15.
Horses and carriages. Good location. Terms moderate.

———◆•◆•◆—— ——

MAHWAH, BERGEN CO., N. J.

**29 Miles from New York: 7 Trains from and 8 Trains
to New York daily; 5 Trains from and 4 to
New York Sunday.**

FARE- LOCAL, 95c.; EXCURSION, $1.25; COMMUTATION, 3 MONTHS, $30.

The beginning of the celebrated Ramapo Valley scenery. Mountain
air, spring water, good drives, cool retreats.

——✻——

SUMMER HOTEL.

MOUNTAIN VIEW HOUSE—DAVID FOX, Proprietor · 1 mile from
depot. Same distance from Suffern. Free transportation in covered
side-seat stage. Accommodations for 60; 7 single rooms; 27 double
rooms; $7 to $10 per week for single room; $11 to $20 per week for
double room; $2 per day. Discount to season guests in some cases.
Can furnish boats and fishing-tackle, gun and dog, at reasonable
charge. Proprietor or his man acts as guide at reasonable rates. Furnishes livery to sportsmen; $5 per day for team and man. General
livery charge, 75 cents to $1.25 per hour. Furnishes a four in-hand
for pleasure driving, at a reasonable charge. Fine croquet ground,
billiard table, etc. Best of references from former guests. Raises
vegetables, fruits, etc. P. O. address, Suffern, N. Y., or Mahwah, N. J.

HOTEL.

MAHWAH HOUSE—A. H. HAGERMAN, Proprietor—Near depot. Accommodations for 20; 8 single rooms; $8 per week. Transient, $1 per
day. Discount to season guests. Equipments for sportsmen without
charge. Raises vegetables.

BOARDING HOUSE.

Mrs. D. W. HOPPER 1 mile from depot. Accommodations for 15;
3 single rooms; 3 double rooms; $8 single, $16 double; Children half
price; $2 per day. No discount. Raises vegetables.

SUFFERN, ROCKLAND CO., N. Y.

32 Miles from New York: 9 Trains from and 11 to
New York daily; 6 Trains from and 5
to New York Sunday.

FARE—LOCAL, $1: EXCURSION (3 DAYS), $1.35: COMMUTATION,
3 MONTHS. $31.

At the base of the southern Highlands of the Hudson, in the rocky pass of the Ramapo, eastern terminus of the Piermont Branch of the Erie. Romantic surroundings. Once Washington's headquarters. Famous ground in the Revolution. High hills on every side. Magnificent views. A resort for sufferers with bronchial and pulmonary affections. Recommended by leading physicians. Many natural curiosities. Boarding houses all first-class. Bass and pickerel fishing. Partridge, quail and woodcock.

— ❦ —

BOARDING HOUSES.

T. W. SUFFERN—Two-thirds of a mile from depot ; 500 feet above sea level. Transportation free. Accommodations for 30 ; 4 single rooms ; 16 double rooms ; $8 to $10 ; $1.50 per day ; discount to season guests. Raises vegetables. Boats and fishing tackle free. Acts as guide to lakes free to guests.

C. A. WANNEMAKER—¾ of a mile from depot. Accommodations for 10. Two double rooms. $6 to $7 per week. Raises vegetables.

A. E. IVERS, Lock Box 6 —Less than ¼ mile from depot. Accommodations for 50 ; 12 single rooms ; 16 double rooms ; $7 to $9 single ; $15 to $18 double. Liberal discount to season guests. Best accommodations for 15 horses. Handsome modern house ; hot and cold water in every room. Grounds 9 acres ; plenty of fruit and vegetables. Attendance and table first-class. Three minutes from boating and fishing.

MOUNTAIN TERRACE HOUSE—Three minutes walk from depot. Accommodations for 60 ; 6 single rooms ; 20 double rooms ; $5 to $10 single ; $10 to $20 double ; $1.50 per day. Discount to season guests. On banks of Ramapo river. Extensive grounds. Shaded lawn. Good water. Boating and fishing on the premises. Room for horses and carriages.

FARM HOUSES.

H. A. WANNEMAKER—Short distance from depot. Transportation free. Accommodations for 10 ; $8 per week. Raises his own vegetables. Ramapo river runs through his premises.

AUGUSTUS COE—2½ miles from depot. Transportation free. Accommodations for 20 ; 4 single rooms ; 2 double rooms ; $6 to $8 ; 50c. per meal. Farm produce.

LAWRENCE D. N. COE—2½ miles from depot. Transportation free. Accommodations for 30 ; 5 single rooms ; 10 double rooms ; $5 to $8 ; 50 cents per meal. Discount to season guests. Furnishes livery. Raises own vegetables on farm.

ABBOTT COOPER—2½ miles from depot. Free transportation. Accommodations for 25 ; $6 to $9 ; $1.50 per day. Good stabling. Lake of 2½ acres running spring water. Boats. Vegetables, fruits, &c., from the farm.

LIVERY.

P. FINNIGAN, J. H. WANNEMAKER, M. D. DURYEA—75 cents an hour ; $3 to $5 per day.

RAMAPO, ROCKLAND CO., N. Y.

34 Miles from New York : 4 Trains from and 3 to
New York daily ; 4 Trains from and 2 to
New York on Sunday.

FARE—LOCAL, $1.05; EXCURSION, $1.40; COMMUTATION, 3 MONTHS, $33.

In the Ramapo Valley. Scenery wild and picturesque. Torne Mountain, from the summit of which the Brooklyn Bridge towers may be seen, is the striking feature of the locality. Good drives to the mountain, Potague Lake Sterling Lake and mines, Truxedo Lake, and up and down the valley. Charming walks and rambles. Best black bass and pickerel fishing in the Ramapo River and the above lakes.

—❈—

BOARDING HOUSE.

TERRACE HALL—A. MACFARLANE, Proprietor—Near depot. Accommodations for 50 ; $1.50 to $2 per day. On Ramapo Lake. Picturesque location. First-class in every respect. Best of references. Favorite spot for artists.

Livery at Suffern.

—◆◆◆◆—

SLOATSBURG, ROCKLAND CO., N. Y.

36 Miles from New York : 4 Trains from and 3 Trains
to New York daily ; 4 Trains from and 2 to
New York Sunday.

FARE—LOCAL, $1.30 ; EXCURSION, $1.75 ; COMMUTATION, 3 MONTHS.
$35.50.

Centre of a famous sporting region. Lorillard's Lake, 3 miles ; Potague Lake, 1 mile ; Cedar Lake, 2 miles ; others in the vicinity. Romantic drives. Bass and pickerel fishing. Lakes from 500 to 1,000 feet above tide. Wild surroundings.

—❈—

HOTEL.

T. J. ALLEN'S—Accommodations for 20 ; $5 to $8.

BOARDING HOUSE.

SLOAT MANSION V. L. TODD, Proprietor—Accommodations for 40; 8 single rooms; 14 double rooms; $7 to $9 single ; $14 to $20 double; $2.50 per day. Discount to season guests. Gas, bath, and billiards. Lawn of 20 acres. Raises vegetables.

8

LORILLARD'S, ROCKLAND CO., N. Y.

39 Miles from New York : 2 Trains to and 1 Train from
New York daily ; 1 Train each
way on Sunday.

FARE - LOCAL, $1.20 ; EXCURSION, $1.60.

STATION FOR LORILLARD'S OR TRUXEDO LAKE Property
of Lorillard estate. One mile from station. 500 feet above tide. Wild
surroundings. Black bass, pickerel and perch. Privilege of fishing, $5
per rod per day, boat included. Conveyance furnished from station to
lake on notice to Josiah Patterson, Sloatsburg, Rockland Co., N. Y.,
50 cents each way. Guide, $2 per day.

◆ ● ◆ ● ◆

SOUTHFIELDS, ROCKLAND CO., N. Y.

42 Miles from New York : 4 Trains each way daily ;
4 Trains from and 2 to New York Sunday.

FARE LOCAL, $1.30; EXCURSION, $1.75; COMMUTATION, 3 MONTHS, $39.

Also a station from which the lakes are readily reached ; Truxedo, 3
miles ; Mambasha, 3 miles. Good roads.

— ※ —

BOARDING HOUSE.

OAK COTTAGE - MRS. SHANKLAND, Proprietor—Short walk from
depot. Free transportation. Accommodations for 35 ; 8 single rooms ;
8 double rooms ; $7 to $10 single ; $16 to $30 double. At base of mountains. Lake on mountain, back of house. Raises vegetables.

LIVERY.

JOHN SPELLER—$2 to $4 per day.

◆ ● ◆ ● ◆

TURNER'S, ORANGE CO., N. Y.

48 Miles from New York : 10 Trains from New York
daily, and 6 on Sunday ; 8 Trains to New
York daily and 6 on Sunday.

FARE—LOCAL, $1.45; EXCURSION, $1.95; COMMUTATION, 3 MONTHS, $42.

(*Change cars for Central Valley, Highland Mills, Woodbury, Moun-
tainville, Cornwall, and Newburgh. see page 33.*)

Last resort in Ramapo Valley. Famous as dining station on Erie
Railway. Finest scenery. Beginning of celebrated Orange county
dairy region. Near all the lakes mentioned, and also those on the Hudson Highlands. Surrounded by mountains. Partridge, quail, woodcock. Slaughter Lake, 3 miles ; Rumsey Lake, 2 miles ; Little Long,
3½ miles ; Mambasha, 4 miles ; Round Lake, 3 miles—bass, pickerel,
perch.

9

BOARDING HOUSES.

Mrs. R. McKELVEY ¾ of mile from depot. Free transportation. Accommodations for 12; 2 single rooms; 4 double rooms; $5 to $7. Discount to season guests. High ground. All the lakes easy of access. Hunting grounds near. Greenwood Lake 10 miles. Furnishing vegetables, fruits, eggs, milk and butter from farm. Will rent the house on reasonable terms.

N. B. STARKWEATHER—½ mile from depot. Accommodations for 25; 14 rooms; $7 to $9. Horses and wagons for use of guests. Farm of 30 acres, 1,000 feet above tide. Vegetables, fruits, eggs, butter, and milk from the farm.

GILBERT TURNER— Accommodations for 20; $6 to $9.

W. C. SMITH—Accommodations for 30; $6 to $8.

F. H. MASTEN—Accommodations for 15; $6 to $10.

C. T. FORD, Jr. (Hotel) Accommodations for 20; $6 to $10

LIVERY.

C. T. FORD, Jr.—Team, per hour, 75 cents; single rig, 50 cents per hour.

———◄•●•►———

MONROE, ORANGE COUNTY, N. Y.

50 Miles from New York: 6 Trains from and 7 to New York daily; 4 Trains each way Sundays.

FARE—LOCAL, $1.55; EXCURSION (3 DAYS), 2.05; COMMUTATION 3 MOS., $44.

Among the dairy farms of Southern Orange. Highest elevation of any station on the Erie, east of Shawangunk Mountains. Lakes, and streams, and mountains. Highlands 2 miles southward. Greenwood Lake, 9 miles. Splendid drives. Monroe, Round, and Long Ponds near. Black bass, pickerel, perch, woodcock, quail, rabbits.

——✳——

HOTELS.

SEVEN SPRINGS MOUNTAIN HOUSE—J. G. DAVIDSON, Proprietor—Two miles from depot. Stages and carriages, 50 cents. Accommodations for 400; 100 single rooms; 100 double rooms; $8 to $15 single; $10 to $20 double; $3 to $5 per day. Discount to season guests. 2,000 feet above tide, near top of Schunemunk Mountain. Fine mountain retreat. Three spacious stone buildings, connected by covered walks. Extended view of most picturesque portion of Orange County. Pure dry air, beneficial in pulmonary complaints. Mineral spring for rheumatism, kidney and liver diseases. Billiards, croquet, archery. Dancing every night. Livery attached. Saddle horses on hire. Stages connect with every train. Best city references.

MONROE HOUSE— J. J. VAN DUZER, Proprietor—Near depot. Accommodations for 50; 20 single rooms; 20 double rooms; $10 single; $20 double; $2 per day. Discount to season guests. Raises vegetables. Guns and dogs. Livery attached. $5 to $10 per day, with guide.

BOARDING HOUSES.

W. R. CONKLING—¾ mile from station. Free transportation. Accommodations for 16; 13 rooms; $6 and $7. Children half price. Parties invited to inspect place. Raises vegetables.

P. C. HAGER—¼ mile from depot. Three single rooms, adjoining, for family; 4 double rooms; $6 to $8. No discount. Furnishes livery, $3 to $5 per day. Boats, 50 cents.

GRANITE HOUSE—Short walk from depot. Accommodations for 10; 20 rooms; $7 to $8. Beautiful lawn. Fine shade. Farm 15 acres. Vegetables, milk, cream, eggs, butter, fruit, all from the farm.

MRS. A. CARPENTER—½ mile from depot. Accommodations for 15; 5 single rooms; 2 double rooms; $7 single; $9 double; 10 cents a meal. Raises vegetables.

FARM HOUSE.

URIAH CROSSON—2½ miles from depot. Transportation 30 cents. Accommodations for 12; 4 single rooms; 4 double rooms; $6 single; $12 double; $1 per day; no discount.

WM. SUTHERLAND—¼ mile from depot. Accommodations for 12; $6; $1.50 per day.

LIVERY.

M. KONNIGHT, J. N. VAN DUZER—$3 per day single rigs; team $5.

GUIDES.

TO LAKES—A. BODENSTIEN—$2 to $3 per day. Boats, 25 cents.

TO HUNTING GROUNDS—H. RIDER, D. REDNER; $2 to $3 per day.

— ◆•◆•◆ —

OXFORD, ORANGE COUNTY, N. Y.

52 Miles from New York: 4 Trains each way daily; 4 Trains from and 3 to New York Sundays.

FARE—LOCAL, $1.60; EXCURSION (3 DAYS), $2.15; COMMUTATION, 3 MOS., $15.50.

Fine scenery, lakes and streams, pure air and water have made this a popular retreat. Greenwood Lake, 9 miles.

— ⁂ —

FARM HOUSES.

JAMES M. SEELY—Accommodations for 20; $5 to $8.

A. H. LAURENCE—Accommodations for 15; $4 to $8.

JOS. W. YOUNGS—Accommodations for 20; $5 to $10.

A. Y. CLARK—Accommodations for 30; $5 to $8.

GREYCOURT, ORANGE COUNTY, N. Y.

54 Miles from New York: 6 Trains from and 7 to
New York daily ; 4 Trains each way Sundays.

FARE LOCAL, $1.65; EXCURSION (3 DAYS), $2.25; COMMUTATION, 3
MOS., $46.50.

(*Change cars for Warwick, Craigville, Washingtonville, Salisbury, and
Newburgh ; see page 13.*)

Junction of the Newburgh and Warwick Branches with the main
line of the Erie. Former follows valley of Murderer's Kill. Other
around base of the Sugar-Loaf Mountain.

—※—

HOTEL.

GREYCOURT HOUSE—JOHN R. PROCTER, Proprietor—Near depot.
Accommodations for 12 : $7 per week. Children half price.

FARM HOUSE.

J. M. SEELEY—One mile from depot. Accommodations for 12 ; $6
to $8 per week. House large and commodious. Milk, eggs, cream,
fresh butter, fruit and vegetables.

→●●●→

CHESTER, ORANGE CO., N. Y.

55 Miles from New York: 6 Trains from and 7 to
New York daily ; 4 Trains each way Sundays.

FARE—LOCAL, $1.70 ; EXCURSION (3 DAYS), $2.30 ; COMMUTATION,
3 MOS., $47.25.

A quiet, agricultural neighborhood. Good drives. Fine scenery.
Methodist and Presbyterian Church. Quail and woodcock. Black bass
and pickerel near.

—※—

OLD-FASHIONED FARM HOUSE.

GEORGE SULLY—1 mile from depot. Accommodations for 6 ; 1
single room; 2 double rooms ; $5 single ; $7 double. Discount to season guests. Streams close by the house. Vegetables and fruits from
farm.

13

GOSHEN, ORANGE CO., N. Y.

59 Miles from New York: 10 Trains from and 11 to
New York daily; 5 Trains from and 6 Trains
to New York Sundays.

FARE—LOCAL, $1.85; EXCURSION 3 DAYS), $2.50; COMMUTATION,
3 Mos., $50.

(*Change cars for Florida ; Lake Mohonk and Lake Minnewaska (New
Paaltz) ; and all resorts under the head of " In the
Catskills" (Kingston), see page 15.*)

One of the oldest places in the State. A shire town of Orange
County. Famous for its butter, milk and blooded horses. Very
wealthy. The stock farms in and near Goshen are celebrated all over
the Union. An interesting locality for summer sojourners and tourists.
Black bass fishing in the Wallkill river and Pochunk Creek. Several
lakes easy of access. Drives excellent. Good livery.

—✲—

HOTELS.

OCCIDENTAL HOTEL.—A. A. BROWNSON, Proprietor—Near depot.
Accommodations for 50. $6 to $10 per week ; $2 per day.

ORANGE HOTEL—JAS. GALWAY, Proprietor—Short walk from depot. Accommodations for 50 ; $6 to $10 per week ; $2 per day.

FARM HOUSE.

J. A. BREWSTER- 2½ miles from depot. Accommodations for 15.
$7 to $10 per week.

LIVERY STABLE.

R. R. CARR, D. VAN SICKLE, J. HINCHMAN—$2 to $6 per
day.

—◆•◆•◆—

FLORIDA, ORANGE CO., N. Y.

5 Miles from Goshen, on Pine Island Branch ; 2
Trains each way daily ; 2 Trains
each way Sundays.

Among meadows and hills. Mount Adam and Mount Eve, two lofty
elevations, near by. Glenmere Lake, one of the handsomest lakes in
the State, is one mile from Florida. Bass fishing. Quail shooting.

—✲—

HOTEL.

DILL HOUSE—ALBERT RANDALL, Proprietor. Near depot. Accommodations for 30 ; 12 single rooms ; 9 double rooms ; $6 and $10 ; $2
per day. Raises and buys vegetables.

MIDDLETOWN, ORANGE CO., N. Y.

67 Miles from New York: 7 Trains from and 9 to New York daily; 4 Trains from and 6 to New York on Sundays.

FARE—LOCAL, $2.05; EXCURSION (3 DAYS), $2.75; COMMUTATION, 3 MOS., $53.

(Change cars at Main street for Ellenville, Fallsburgh, and Stations on the Midland Railroad; see page 24.)

The handsomest village on the Eastern Division. Population, about 9,000. Presbyterian, Methodist, Congregational, Baptist, Episcopal, Catholic, and Free Christian churches. Clean, broad streets, pure water, perfect drainage, sanitary condition unsurpassed. Fine residences and beautiful grounds. Best drives in the county. Surroundings, hills, woods, and valleys. Two daily newspapers. In the heart of the Orange County dairy region. Pickerel and bass fishing in the Wallkill. Trout streams of Sullivan County easy of access. Woodcock and quail shooting. Junction of Midland Railroad.

—⁂—

PRIVATE HOUSES.

CHARLES Z. TAYLOR—⅓ mile from depot. Transportation, 10 cents. Accommodations for 3; 1 single room; 1 double room; $6, single; $10, double. New house, high location, fine view. Raises and buys vegetables.

MRS. S. L. PRESTON—5 minutes walk from either depot. Omnibus transfer, 10 cents. Accommodations for 5; 5 single rooms; 1 double room; $5, single, $8, double; $1 per day. Raises and buys vegetables.

BOARDING HOUSES.

DAVID R. MILLER—⅓ mile from depot. Free transportation. Accommodations for 20; 5 single rooms; 3 double rooms; $6; children half price. Splendid location in corporation limits. House new. Furnishes livery. Raises vegetables.

LIVERY STABLES.

A. J. BRINK'S, AT TAYLOR HOUSE: LEWIS SCOTT'S, A. J. HERRICK, A. WILKINSON, $3 to $6 per day.

14

HOWELL'S, ORANGE CO., N. Y.

71 Miles from New York: 3 Trains from and 4 to New York daily; 3 Trains each way Sundays.

FARE—LOCAL, $2.20; EXCURSION (3 DAYS), $2.90; COMMUTATION, 3 Mos., $55.75.

A hamlet in the famous dairy region. Beautiful rolling country. Splendid outlook to the Shawangunk range. Quiet and healthful. Congregational Church. Woodcock in season.

——✳——

FARM HOUSE.

ALBERT MAPES—1 mile from depot. Free transportation. Accommodations for 8; 3 single rooms, to accommodate 2 each; 1 double room, large parlor and bedroom, for 2; $5 and $8; $1.00 per day. Livery in Middletown, 3 miles. Vegetables, milk, butter, and eggs in abundance.

——◆◆◆◆——

OTISVILLE, ORANGE CO., N. Y.

76 Miles from New York: 3 Trains from and 4 to New York daily; 3 Trains each way Sundays.

FARE—LOCAL, $2.35; EXCURSION (3 DAYS), $3.10; COMMUTATION, 3 Mos., $58.50.

A quiet farming neighborhood, in the midst of the dairies. 1,200 feet above tide, on the summit of the Shawangunk range. A magnificent outlook in all directions. Woodcock shooting in season.

——✳——

PRIVATE HOUSES.

MRS. J. H. REED—Short walk from depot. Accommodations for 12; 4 single rooms; 4 double rooms; $6; $1 per day. Raises vegetables.

15

MRS. M. O. WILKIN—3 minutes walk from depot. Accommodations for 6; 3 double rooms, or suite of 4, suitable for family or party; $5; $1 per day. No discount for season. Half mile from summit of Shawangunk mountains. Raises vegetables.

W. C. TYMESON—¾ mile from depot. Free transportation. Accommodations for 30; 8 single rooms; 5 double rooms; $6. single; $10, double; $1 per day. Large grounds. Lake on the premises. Free boats. Raises vegetables.

FARM HOUSE.

S. BERTHOLF—1 mile from depot. Free transportation. Accommodations for 12; 6 rooms; 2 may be used single or double; $6 to $8. No transient rate. No discount. Old-fashioned farm. Fine locality.

HOTELS.

LEMONS HOUSE—J. B. LEMONS, Proprietor. Near depot. Accommodations for 20; $6 to $10; $2 per day. Discount to season guests.

GREEN'S HOTEL—O. B. GREEN, Proprietor. Near depot. Accommodations for 20; $6 to $10, $2 per day. Discount to season guests.

LIVERY.

BLIZARD HOUSE STABLES—$3 per day, single rigs; teams, $5.

—•◄•►•—

GUYMARD, ORANGE CO., N. Y.

LOCAL FARE, $2.45; EXCURSION (3 DAYS), $3.30; COMMUTATION, 3 MONTHS, $61.00.

In the Shawangunk Mountains. A wild retreat, and popular with city people.

—※—

HOTEL.

GUYMARD SPRINGS MOUNTAIN HOUSE—Near depot. Accommodations for 100; 20 single rooms; 30 double rooms $12.50 single; $20 to $30 double—$3 per day. Discount to season guests. 1,200 feet above tide-water. Neversink river near. Vegetables raised in vicinity.

PORT JERVIS, ORANGE CO., N. Y.

87 Miles from New York: 6 Trains from New York;
6 Trains to New York, daily; 3 Trains from
New York; 4 Trains to New York
Sunday.

FARE—LOCAL, $2.70; EXCURSION (3 DAYS), $3.60; COMMUTATION,
3 MOS., $65.

*(Change cars for Monticello and White Lake; stages for Milford and
Dingman's Ferry; see page 18.)*

Population, 9,000. Terminus of the Eastern and Delaware Divisions of the Erie Railway. Junction of the Port Jervis and Monticello Railroad. Station for Milford, Pa., Dingman's Ferry, Pa., and all the Lower Delaware Valley resorts. Beautifully located on the Delaware and Neversink rivers, in the midst of the finest scenery. The famous trout streams, bass and pickerel lakes, and hunting grounds of Pike and Sullivan counties are reached from Port Jervis. Best of bass-fishing in the Delaware, at the village. Unsurpassed drives. The high peaks surrounding this place afford extended views of the surroundings for more than 100 miles. Presbyterian, Methodist, Reformed, Baptist, Lutheran, Episcopal, and Catholic churches. Good schools. Gas and water works. A cultured and hospitable population. Hotels first-class. The region was one of the earliest settled in the country. Fine field for antiquarian research.

HOTEL.

DELAWARE HOUSE—J. E. WICKHAM, Proprietor. Opposite depot. Accommodations for 150; 100 single rooms; 25 double rooms; $2 per day. Discount to season guests. Broad piazzas. Coach office for Milford and places in the Delaware valley. Furnishes guides to lakes and streams, free to guests. Half a mile from best Delaware bass-fishing grounds. Livery attached. Vegetables all fresh from hotel gardens.

LIVERY STABLES.

QUICK & HULSIZER—DELAWARE HOUSE; JAMES BUCHANAN, B. GODLEY, T. MAGUIRE, E. SLAUSON; $3 to $5 per day. Conveyance to Milford—single, $2; team $4. To Dingman's—single, $3; team, $6.

IN THE LOWER DELAWARE VALLEY.

———— ◆ ————

MILFORD, PIKE CO., PA.

A Splendid Drive of 7 Miles from Port Jervis, down the Delaware Valley.

County-seat of the famous Pike County. Situated on a high bluff overlooking the Delaware river. Surrounded by mountains. Streets broad, free from dust, densely shaded, and hard as cement. The centre of a celebrated trout, bass and pickerel fishing, and deer, bear, partridge and woodcock region. The remarkable waterfalls on the Sawkill, Raymondskill, Sanvantine and Vandermark Creeks, are from one to three miles from village. There are not less than 100 of these falls, from 20 to 100 feet in height, and set in the midst of the wildest surroundings. Milford Glen on the Sawkill, is a cool retreat in the village. Sawkill Pond, Little Log Tavern Pond, Big and Little Walker Ponds, and Brink Pond are from 4 to 10 miles distant. Best of black bass and trout fishing almost within the bounds of the village. Hotels and boarding houses are all first-class. Presbyterian, Methodist, Episcopal, and Catholic churches. The drives are not surpassed by any city boulevard. The river road, from Port Jervis to Bushkill, 30 miles, is as smooth as a floor. Livery accommodations are excellent.

—— ❖ ——

HOTELS.

FAUCHERE HOUSE—L. Fauchere, Proprietor—Stage from Port Jervis. House erected this season on site of former hotel ; open June 1. Accommodations for 100 ; 15 single rooms ; 25 double rooms ; $14 single ; $28 to $30 double, according to room ; $2.50 per day. House three stories, 50x75 feet. Central location. French style. Modern cottages attached. Vegetables raised on the premises and in the vicinity.

CRISSMAN HOUSE—Frank Crissman, Proprietor—Stage from Port Jervis. Accommodations for 75 ; 15 single rooms ; 30 double rooms ; $7 to $9 single ; $16 to $18 double ; $2 per day. Discount to season guests. Billiard parlor. Commodious stables. Fresh vegetables, milk, butter, and eggs from farm.

SAWKILL HOUSE—John Cornelius, Proprietor—Stage from Port Jervis. Accommodations for 60 ; 14 single rooms ; 18 double rooms ; $10 single ; $20 double ; $2 per day. Discount to season guests. Patronized by leading families of New York, Brooklyn and Philadelphia. Raises vegetables.

RIVER VIEW HOUSE - F. LeClerc, Proprietor - Transports guests from Port Jervis on notice. Accommodations for 40; 4 single rooms; 10 double rooms; $12 single; $24 double; $2 per day. Discount to season guests. Overlooks Delaware river. Large grounds; summer houses. Pleasant cottages attached; French style. Large garden. Fine location.

GUSTAVE DE BEHRL'S—Stage from Port Jervis. Accommodations for 50; 18 single rooms; 12 double rooms; $10 to $12 single, according to floor; $12 double. Equips sportsmen. Boats and tackle $1 a day. On banks of Delaware. French cooking. Large garden. Spring water on every floor.

BOARDING HOUSES.

BLUFF HOUSE—H. B. Wells & John Van Campen, Proprietors—Stage from Port Jervis. Accommodations for 100; 40 single rooms; 25 double rooms; $8 to $15 single; $16 to $30 double; $2 per day. Discount to season guests. On banks of Delaware. 150 feet above. Extended view of valley. Broad verandas and balconies. Spring water throughout. Bath rooms. Four acres of grounds fronting on river. Raises vegetables.

BARNES COTTAGE—H. Barnes, Proprietor—Stage. Accommodations for 40; 15 single rooms; 5 double rooms; $7 single; $7 to $8 double; $1.50 per day. Discount to season guests. One of the most pleasant locations in town. Milford Glen in the rear of the grounds. Rooms cool and airy. Vegetables and fruits from the grounds and vicinity. Table celebrated. Best city references.

GLEN COTTAGE—Emile Reviere, Proprietor—Stage from Port Jervis. Accommodations for 30; 11 double rooms; $10 to $12 single; $11, $12, $14 double; $2 and $2.50 per day. Discount to season guests. Near famous Milford Glen. French style.

J. J. RYMAN—Stage from Port Jervis. Accommodations for 15; 1 single room; 8 double rooms; $7 single; $8 to $10 double; $2 per day. Discount to season guests. Raises vegetables.

COUNTRY HOME—E. L. Van Etten, Proprietor—12 miles from Port Jervis. P. O. address, Box 182, Milford, Pa. Private conveyance or stage $1. Accommodations for 12; 4 single rooms; 4 double rooms; $7; $1.25 per day. Discount to season guests. Near all the waterfalls. The celebrated Conashaugh Spring on the place. Milk, eggs and vegetables fresh every day.

LIVERY.

J. SCHORR, JOHN FINDLAY, GEO. HORTON. $3 to $10 per day, according to number and distance. Single rigs $3 per day. Will meet passengers at Port Jervis on notice by telegraph or mail. Single rig $2; team $5.

GUIDES.

JOHN SLACK, B. BENNETT, JOHN HANS, GEORGE HANS, I. BOYD. $1.50 per day.

STAGE LINES.

Two lines connect with all trains at Port Jervis, day and night, during summer season. Day fare, 50 cents; night fare, 75 cents.

19

DINGMAN'S FERRY, PIKE CO., PA.

15 Miles from Port Jervis. Stage connection. Fare $1.

A resort in a part of the Delaware Valley the character of whose surroundings have given it the name of the Switzerland of America. It is a region of cataracts, mountains, glens, gorges, and wonderful lakes. Dingman's Creek, Adams' Brook, and Decker's Creek, are successions of precipitous waterfalls for miles. Eight of these are within 2 miles of the village. The mountain drives are equal to those of the Catskills. The streams are famous for their trout. The lakes and Delaware river afford the best of bass and pickerel fishing.

--- ※ ---

HOTELS.

HIGH FALLS HOUSE — Philip F. Fulmer, M. D., Proprietor—Stage from Port Jervis, or will meet guests at train if notified. Accommodations for 160 ; 50 single rooms : 55 double rooms ; $10 ; $2 per day. Hunting and fishing parties, $8 ; $1.50 per day. Children and servants half price. Discount to season guests. Open May 1. Spring water. Table supplied from hotel garden. Rooms spacious and airy. Best references in New York, Brooklyn, Philadelphia and other cities.

RAN. VAN CORDEN'S Stage from Port Jervis, or will meet guests on notice. Accommodations for 15 ; 8 single rooms ; 4 double rooms ; $8 single ; $7 double ; $1.25 per day. Fresh vegetables, milk, butter and eggs from the farm daily. Table celebrated.

BELLEVUE HOUSE—James Fuick, Proprietor —Stage, or private conveyance on notice. Accommodations for 50 ; 8 single rooms ; 21 double rooms ; $10 single ; $10 to $14 double ; $1.50 per day. Discount to season guests. French style. Guides from the house. Boats free. Vegetables from the hotel garden.

Among the Sullivan and Ulster Mountains.

MONTICELLO, SULLIVAN CO., N. Y.

5 Hours Ride from New York, via Erie Railway to
Port Jervis, thence by Port Jervis and Monticello Railroad.   Close Connections,
from Erie Depot.

Population 1,200. Elevation of 1,700 feet above tide. County seat of
Sullivan County. Most romantic scenery in the State. Surrounded by
lakes, trout streams, and game preserves. Pleasant Lake, 1 mile ; Sack-
ett, 4 miles ; White Lake, 9 miles ; Black Lake, 9 miles ; furnish best
of bass, pickerel and perch fishing. The trout streams are near by.
Guides $1 per day. Deer, bear, foxes, partridge, quail, woodcock,
English snipe, duck, wild pigeons in season. No malaria or fever. A
mosquito was never seen in Monticello. Streets wide, clean, and well-
shaded. Fine residences and grounds. Much wealth and culture.
Waterfalls and other natural attractions in the vicinity. Paved walks.
Unsurpassed views. A beautiful public park. Hotels and boarding
houses first-class in all respects.

— ※ —

HOTEL.

MANSION HOUSE LE GRAND MORRIS, Proprietor—¼ mile from
depot. Free omnibus. Accommodations for 125 ; 45 single rooms ;
30 double rooms ; $6 to $8 ; $2 per day. Discount to season guests.
Everything modern. Location central and pleasant. Rooms large,
nicely furnished, ceilings high. Particular attention to table ser-
vice. Best city references. Equips sportsmen free of charge. Fresh
farm products. House highly recommended

BOARDING HOUSES.

WM. J. LAWSON, P. O. Box 205—2½ miles from depot. Stage or
private conveyance. Accommodations for 25 ; 14 large rooms ; terms
according to room and number occupying it ; $1 per day. Farm
attached.

TOWNER'S VILLA—Mrs. R. B. Towner, Proprietress—½ mile from depot. Omnibus for every train, 10 cents. Accommodations for 30; 5 single rooms; 9 double rooms; $8 to $10; $1.50 per day. Liberal discount to season guests. House finely situated. Attractive grounds. High location. Grove in rear of grounds. Raises vegetables.

A. S. LANDFIELD—½ mile from depot. Omnibus. Accommodations for 28; 10 single rooms; 9 double rooms; $6 to $8 single; $7 to $10 double; $2 per day. Discount to season guests. Thirty acres of grounds. Plenty of shade. Raises vegetables.

MRS. ELSIE KRUM—¾ mile from depot. Accommodations for 6; ladies preferred; $5 to $7. Use of piano and parlor. Fine location.

N. L. STERN—¼ mile from depot. Coach 10 cents. Accommodations for 15; 3 single rooms; 6 double rooms; $8 to $10 single; $16 to $20 double; $1.50 per day. Discount to season guests. Raises vegetables.

MRS. CHAS. BURNHAM—¼ mile from depot. Accommodations for 10; 2 single rooms; 3 double rooms; $6 and $7; $1 per day. Raises vegetables.

W. H. & H. B. REYNOLDS—3 miles from depot. Conveyance. Accommodations for 20; $5; no discount. Raise vegetables.

FARM HOUSES.

J. D. W. COULTER—1½ miles from depot. Free transportation. Accommodations for 12; 5 single rooms; 2 double rooms; $6 single; $12 to $14 double. High ground. Mail twice a day. Had some guests five successive seasons.

JOHN HILL—2 miles from depot, on White Lake road. Stage. Accommodations for 15; rooms large; $5 to $7. Plenty of shade. Large grounds. Fresh vegetables, milk, butter, eggs from farm.

MRS. E. TOOHEY—Near Barnum's depot, Port Jervis and Monticello R. R., 4 miles from Monticello. Accommodations for 18; $6. Reduction to families. Pickerel and trout fishing near. Mail daily. Vegetables, etc., fresh from farm.

GEO. MAPLEDORAM—Near depot. Accommodations for 8; 2 must room together; $5 the lowest rate. Romantic and sightly location. Shaded walks and retreats.

GEO. W. DECKER—2¼ miles from depot. Free transportation on notice. Accommodations for 20; $6 to $8 single; $12 double. Best city references. Produce from the farm.

A. D. SMITH—3 miles from depot. Free transportation on notice. Accommodations for 20; 5 single rooms; 5 double rooms; $6.

PRIVATE RESIDENCES.

MRS. H. MENZIES—¼ mile from depot. Accommodations for 12; 2 single rooms ; 5 double rooms--$6 to $8. Discount to season guests.

GEO. McLAUGHLIN—¾ mile from village. Accommodations for 8. Ladies without children preferred- $5 to $7. Use of piano. Croquet ground. Large house, pleasant rooms. Shady walks.

LIVERY STABLES.

A. D. O'NEIL, STURDEVANT'S, and KENNEDY'S. $2 to $5 per day. Sportsmen two-thirds regular rates. Accommodations first-class.

◄ ● ◆ ● ►

WHITE LAKE, SULLIVAN CO., N. Y.

9 Miles from Monticello: Stages connect with every Train at that place ; Fare to Lake, $1.

The largest of the many lakes of Sullivan County ; 1,500 feet above tide, and surrounded by the finest mountain scenery ; 14 miles from the Delaware Valley at Cochecton. The lake is stocked with all kinds of game fish. The black bass are marvels of size and flavor. The lake is surrounded by first-class boarding houses. The air is similar to that in the Hudson Highlands. Has been a popular resort for 30 years.

—※—

BOARDING HOUSES.

LAKE SHORE COTTAGE—JOHN CORBY, Proprietor—Eight miles from Monticello. Stage or private conveyance, $1. Accommodations for 33 ; 2 single rooms ; 22 double rooms ; $7 per week for single room; $14 for two persons, double room. House on the western shore of the lake. Free boats. No guide required. Furnishes guns, dogs, &c. Raises fruits and vegetables.

VAN WERT HOUSE—VAN WERT BROS., Proprietors—7½ miles from Monticello. Stage and private conveyance, $1. Accommodations for 75 ; 20 single rooms ; 20 double rooms ; $8 per week for single room ; $16 for double ; $1.50 per day. Raise vegetables.

MANSION HOUSE—D. B. KINNE, Proprietor—Nine miles from Monticello depot. Transportation in stage and private conveyance, $1. Accommodations for 100 ; 15 single rooms ; 35 double rooms ; $7 to $10 per week ; transient, $1.50 per day. Boats, 25 cents. Raises and buys vegetables.

MRS. S. B. KIRK—Eight miles from Monticello. Stage, $1. Accommodations for 30 ; 11 double rooms, adapted for families ; $8 to $10 per week ; transient, $2 per day. Provides boats, not fishing-tackle ; no charge. No guides needed. Vegetables raised on the farm.

SUNNY GLADE HOUSE -WM. WADDELL, Proprietor—Eight miles from Monticello. Stage, $1. Accommodations for 20 ; $8 and $10 per week ; transient, $1.50 per day. Boats free and to let. Raises vegetables.

23

ELLENVILLE, ULSTER CO., N. Y.

90 Miles from New York, via Erie Railway to Middletown, thence via Midland Railroad.

This entire region is among the highest peaks of the Shawangunks, and in the heart of the Ulster and Sullivan trout and pickerel fishing. Ellenville is a charming village. Sam's Point, 6 miles; Lake Minnewaski, 7 miles; the Ice Caves, 1 to 3 miles; Honk Falls, 2 miles, are notable resorts and curiosities.

—❈—

HOTEL.

TERWILLIGER HOUSE—A. CONSTABLE, Proprietor—½ mile from depot. Free omnibus. Accommodations for 50; 45 single rooms; 6 double rooms; $7 single; $10 double; $2 per day. Discount to season guests. First-class house. Livery.

BOARDING HOUSES.

TERRACE HILL—J. A. MEYERS, Proprietor—½ mile from depot. Meets guests at depot if notified. Accommodations for 20; $5 to $7; $1 per day. Raises vegetables.

J. F. RHINEHART--P. O. address: Napanock, Ulster Co., N. Y.— 2 miles from depot. Free transportation. Accommodations for 15; 6 single rooms; 3 double rooms; $5 single; $10 double; $1 per day. Discount to season guests. A trouting and gunning centre. C. Bennett and E. Thorp, fishing guides. O. Wagner hunting guide. $1 per day; furnishing tackle, dogs, and guns. Livery attached; $3 to $5 per day. Raises vegetables.

BENJAMIN VERNOOY—5 miles from Ellenville. P. O. address: Greenfield, Ulster Co., N. Y. Transportation free on notice. Accommodations for 20; 12 single rooms; 4 double rooms; $6 and $7; 2 to 4 in a room; $1 each per day. Pickerel and perch fishing; East, Cape, and Cranberry Lakes; boats 25 cents for 2 persons; no guides needed. Ducks, partridge.

FARM HOUSES.

HILLSDALE HOME—EDGAR VERNOOY, Proprietor. P. O. address: Wawarsing, Ulster Co., N. Y. 7 miles from Ellenville. Free transportation once coming and going; meets guests on notice. Accommodations for 12; no discount. Best trout stream in the country near house; partridge and other small game. House 993 feet above tide. Surrounded by mountains and streams.

S. BURHANS 7 miles from Ellenville. Meets guests on notice; free transportation once coming and going. Accommodations for 8; $5. Trout stream and small game.

LIVERY.

J. PEYO, JAMES THOMPSON, Ellenville—$3 per day, single rigs; $6 team

C. L. WINANT, WILLIAM BRUCE, Greenfield—$2 per day.

FALLSBURGH, SULLIVAN CO., N. Y.

6 Miles from Ellenville Junction of Midland.

MUTTON HILL FARM-HOUSE—O. W. BLOXHAM, Proprietor—
P. O. address: Neversink, Sullivan Co., N. Y. 10 miles from depot.
Free transportation on notice. Accommodations for 26; 3 single rooms;
10 double rooms, 2 for 2 beds each; $6; $1 per day; discount to season
guests. Trouting in Neversink and other streams; pickerel and perch
in North, Gand, and Sheldrake Lakes. Partridge and other small
game; dog and gun. High ground; farm attached. Best city refer-
ence.

——※——

GUIDES,

A. CRYSES, S. SMITH, ELI GARRETT; $1 per day.

LIVERY.

H. DEAN, J. LAWRENCE—$2 per day, single rig; team $4.

—— ◆◆●◆◆ ——

LAKES MOHONK AND MINNEWASKA.

Via Erie Railway to Goshen; thence via Montgomery Branch and Wallkill Valley Branch to New Paaltz; thence via Stage or Carriage.

Amongst the highest and raggedest peaks of the Shawangunk mountains, in Ulster County, N. Y., where only a few years since the foot of
man had seldom trod, are a number of most remarkable and charming
lakes. One of these, Lake Mohonk, has been accessible for several
years, and tourists and permanent summer guests have found an excellent stopping place at the large hotel there. Two years ago Lake Minnewaska was made a summer resort. It is on the rocky crest of a
Shawangunk peak, near "Sam's Point," the great height that overlooks
the entire Wallkill Valley, immediately beneath it, and commands an
unobstructed view of the greater part of the Eastern and Middle States.
They are reached by a most enjoyable drive, on a highway that commands as many wonderful glimpses of scenery as any of the famous
White Mountain drives. Bass and pickerel fishing.

——※——

HOTELS.

AT MOHONK.—Mohonk Lake House, nine miles from New Paaltz
Accommodation for 200; $15 to $20; $3.50 per day. Boats, livery,
telegraph office. No liquors.

AT MINNEWASKA.—Minnewaska Heights House, sixteen miles
from New Paaltz, seven miles from Ellenville. Accommodation for 200;
$15 to $20; $3.50 per day. Boats, livery, telegraph office. No liquors

Professor Smiley, Proprietor of both Hotels. Mail daily.

AMONG THE DELAWARE HIGHLANDS.

SHOHOLA, PIKE CO., PA.

107 Miles from New York: 1 Train from and 2
Trains to New York daily: 1 Train to New
York Sundays.

FARE, $3.30; EXCURSION (4 DAYS), $4.70.

On the banks of the Delaware, 1,000 feet above the sea. In the midst
of the most romantic Pike and Sullivan county scenery. Shohola Glen,
one mile from the station, is a wonderful collection of gorges, waterfalls, precipices, and deep pools. It has been pronounced equal to the
famous Watkins Glen. The Shohola Creek, a celebrated trout stream,
enters the Delaware at this place. Panther Brook, another trout stream,
with several fine cataracts, comes in a short distance above. The Falls
of the Shohola are another attraction. There are nine mountain lakes
reached easily from Shohola, the farthest 6 miles. They are Hagan,
Hagai, Big, Montgomery, Sand and York, in Sullivan County, and
Brink and Big and Little Walker in Pike County, all stocked with bass
and pickerel. Bass fishing in the Delaware. Deer, bear, fox, rabbit,
partridge, and woodcock shooting. Romantic walks and drives.

Shohola is the station from which the most picturesque portion of
Sullivan County is reached. This is in the vicinity of Eldred, among
the Sullivan Highlands and lakes, 1,800 feet above tide. A drive of five
miles from Shohola.

— :·: —

HOTEL.

SHOHOLA HOUSE—GEO. LAYMAN, Proprietor—Near depot. Accommodations for 25; 13 rooms; $8; $1.50 per day. Discount to season
guests. Overlooks river. Near Glen. Broad piazzas. Furnishes livery. Raises vegetables.

FARM BOARDING HOUSES.

ISAAC M. BRADLEY, P. O. Address, Eldred, Sullivan Co., N. Y.—
Five miles from depot. Carriage, single passenger, $2; more than one,
$1. Accommodations for 20; 9 single rooms; 2 double rooms; $7;
$1.50 per day. Centre of trout, bass and pickerel fishing. Boats free.
Deer, bear, partridge, rabbit, woodcock, and wild pigeon shooting.
Deer-hounds and setters furnished, $2 per day. Croquet ground. Meet
parties at Shohola when notified. Best references. Headquarters for
sportsmen. Fresh vegetables, milk, eggs and butter.

MRS. J. A. MEYERS, P. O. Address, Eldred, Sullivan Co., N. Y.—
Five miles from depot, at Highland Lake. Accommodations for 30; $6
to $8. Fine drives. Fresh vegetables, milk, butter and eggs.

LIVERY.

AT SHOHOLA—G. Layman, J. M. Austin, C. Thomas. Terms reasonable.

AT ELDRED— J. M. Bradley. $2 to $3 per day.

GUIDES.

AT ELDRED —J. M. Bradley, Geo. Dunlap, Daniel Hallock. $2 per day.

———— ✦•◆•✦ ————

LACKAWAXEN, PIKE CO., PA.

111 Miles from New York: 3 Trains from and 3 Trains to New York daily. 1 Train from and 2 Trains to New York Sundays.

FARE—LOCAL, $3.40; EXCURSION (5 DAYS), $5.

Change cars for Rowland, Millville (Blooming Grove Park). Kimble's, Hawley, and Honesdale ; see page 10.)

A picturesque spot on the Delaware and Lackawaxen rivers, in northeastern Pennsylvania, in the hunting and fishing region of Pike and Wayne Counties, Pa., and Sullivan County, N. Y. Surrounded by mountains and forests, streams and lakes. York Lake, on the summit of the Sullivan County Highlands, 1,500 feet above tide, is but one mile distant. Wescoline Lake is four miles. The Delaware is formed into a broad lake by the Delaware and Hudson Canal Company's dam at Lackawaxen. Unexcelled boating and bass-fishing. Romantic waterfalls on the New York side of the river. Trout streams—Lord's Brook, one mile ; Panther Brook, one mile ; Taylor's Brook, five miles ; Shohola Creek, six miles ; Beaver Brook, three miles ; Booming Grove and its streams, lakes, and hunting grounds, twelve miles, over a good road. Deer, bear, partridge, woodcock ; bass, trout, pickerel, perch, eels, cat-fish. The famous Delaware shad run up as far as Lackawaxen in their season. No mosquitoes or malaria.

—— ✖ ——

HOTELS.

DELAWARE HOUSE—MRS. M A. HOLBERT, Proprietor; F. J. HOLBERT, Agent —1-3 of a mile from depot. On the banks of the Delaware, at the junction of the Lackawaxen. Transportation free. Accommodations for 100 ; 15 single rooms ; 50 double rooms ; $8 to $12 ; $2 per day. Discount to season guests. Two cottages attached. Grand view

27

up and down the valley. Boating for a mile on the river. Black bass fishing in front of the house. Boats free. Livery furnished ; $5 per day team. Best of references. Fresh vegetables, butter, eggs, milk. etc., from farm.

WILLIAMSON HOUSE—W. B. Dimmick, Proprietor—Near depot. Accommodations for 40 ; 15 single rooms ; 5 double rooms ; $7 to $8 single ; contract for double ; $2 per day. Cottage near. High ground. Grounds of grove and forest. Near all the points of interest. Everything first-class. Broad piazzas. Dogs and equipment for hunters. Furnish horses.

VAN BENSCHOTEN HOUSE C. Van Benschoten, Proprietor— Near depot. Highest ground in the place. Accommodations for 15 ; 6 single rooms ; 4 double rooms ; $10; $1.60 per day. No discount. Furnishes horse and buggy, $3 per day. Boats, 50 cents per day. Vegetables raised on place and in vicinity.

GUIDES.

J. McKAIN—$2 per day. Fishing and hunting.

Sportsmen will find accommodations at John Munson's, Wescoline Lake ; Wm. McCarty, Shohola Falls ; M. C. Westbrook, Blooming Grove.

———— •◦•◦• ————

NARROWSBURG, SULLIVAN CO., N. Y.

128 Miles from New York; 3 Trains from New York, 4 Trains to New York daily ; 1 Train from New York and 3 to New York Sundays.

Fare $3.75 ; Excursion (5 days), $5.75.

On the Delaware river at Big Eddy. No more romantic locality in the valley. Big Eddy is the widest and deepest part of the Delaware river above tide, and is literally a large lake of pure spring water. Black bass fishing unsurpassed. Excellent boating for two miles. Ten mountain lakes within eight miles. Numerous trout streams in the vicinity. No mosquitoes or malaria. Air beneficial in hay fever and asthma. Cool nights. Deer hunting on the surrounding ridges. Partridge shooting good. Splendid drives. A leading dining station at the Erie Railway. A region of interesting legends.

HOTELS.

MURRAY'S HOTEL—C. H. & C. J. Murray, Proprietors. Near depot. Accommodations for fifty: 15 single rooms, 6 double rooms; $7; $2.50 per day. No discount. Rooms large and airy. Broad piazza. Everything first class. Good references. Also proprietors of dining hall in depot.

GEBHARD'S HOTEL—J. Gebhard, Proprietor. Near depot. Accommodations for fifteen; $7; $1.50 per day.

G. UGHLING'S HOTEL. (German.) Accommodations for twenty.

PRIVATE COTTAGE.

WILLOUGHBY COTTAGE—(Old Corwin Homestead)—John D. Ruff, Proprietor. Short walk from depot. Accommodations for boarders at $6. Beautifully located on banks of the river at Big Eddy. Handsomest Homestead on upper Delaware. Fine grounds. Fruit and vegetables.

FARM BOARDING HOUSE.

JOHN ENGLEMAN, one-fourth mile from depot. Near river. Accommodations for twelve; $6. No day boarders. Large, quiet farmhouse.

———→•◆•→———

COCHECTON, SULLIVAN CO., N. Y.

129 Miles from New York : 1 Train from, 2 Trains to New York daily 1 Train to New York Sundays.

FARE, $1 ; EXCURSION (5 DAYS), $6.20.

Quiet village on the Delaware. Settled in 1752. Romantic location. Village of Damascus, Wayne County, Pa., opposite. Very healthful. No malaria or mosquitoes. Swago Lake, 2 miles. Lake Huntington, 4 miles, affords best bass and pickerel fishing. Trout also in Lake Huntington. Bass in Delaware. Calkins Creek, 3 miles, trouting. Accommodations for parties at the lakes. Methodist, Baptist, and Presbyterian churches. Scene of incidents in J. Fennimore Cooper's novels.

HOTEL.

KNAPP HOUSE—DeWITT KNAPP, Proprietor—Opposite depot. Accommodations for 20 ; 10 single rooms ; 5 double rooms ; $5 to $10 single ; $6 to $12 double ; $1.75 per day. Discount to season guests. Vegetables from farm.

BOARDING HOUSE.

LEROY BONESTEEL, P. O. Address, Damascus, Wayne Co., Pa. —¼ mile from depot. Free transportation. Accommodations for 8 ; 2 single rooms ; 3 double rooms ; $5 single ; $7 double. Near Swago, Cline, Baird's, and Laurel Lakes. Bass and pickerel fishing and trout stream. Raises vegetables.

CALLICOON, SULLIVAN CO., N. Y.

186 Miles from New York: 3 Trains from and 2
Trains to New York Daily ; 1 Train from
New York Sunday.

FARE, $4.15 ; EXCURSION (5 DAYS), $6.50.

The immediate surroundings of Callicoon are of the wild and rugged
character that prevails in the upper Delaware Highlands, but a few
minutes' ride will take the visitor to the valley of the Callicoon Creek,
which is for miles a continuation of splendid farms. Callicoon
village is the centre of one of the famous trout regions of the Delaware Valley. The Callicoon Creek, which enters the Delaware a short
distance below the station, threads the back wilderness and the
splendid farming section mentioned. Along its entire course, from the
hills on either side, tributary streams flow into it at short intervals.
The main stream and its feeders are natural trout creeks, and all the
season long they afford royal sport to the angler. These brooks are
within an area of five miles from the station. On the Pennsylvania side
of the river is Hollister Creek. For two miles from the river this creek
flows through a wild and narrow gorge, and seeks the level of the river
by a series of wonderful waterfalls. There are numerous lakes on both
sides of the river, the famous Bethel township lakes, in Sullivan
County, being within easy reach. In Wayne County, Gallilee Lake,
Duck Harbor, Swago Lake, and others, are near and convenient of
access. Bass, pickerel, and perch fishing are attractions of these waters.
Callicoon Depot and Callicoon are different post offices.

---※---

HOTELS.

MINARD HOUSE Z. MINARD, Proprietor—P. O. Address, Callicoon Depot, Sullivan Co., N. Y. Near depot. Accommodations for 30 ;
25 single rooms ; 10 double rooms ; $7 and $8 ; $1.50 per day. Discount
to season guests. Provides boats, guns, and dogs, $1.50 per day. Liv-
ery connected with house—$2 per day for single rigs ; $1 per team.
Plenty of fresh vegetables from hotel gardens.

WESTERN HOTEL MRS L. THORWELLE, Proprietress—P. O. Address, Callicoon Depot. Near depot. Accommodations for 40 ; 10
single rooms ; 6 double rooms ; $6 to $10 single ; $10 to $15 double ;
$1.50 per day. Discount to season guests. Raises vegetables.

FALL MILL HOUSE E. R. LAWRENCE, Proprietor—P. O. Address,
Fall Mills, Sullivan Co., N. Y. 4½ miles from depot. Will meet guests
at train. Accommodations for 25 ; $1 to $8. On the east branch of Callicoon Creek. Best trout fishing and hunting. Large farm attached.
Will give full information by mail on application.

CALLICOON HOTEL—JOHN LUDWIG, Proprietor—P. O. Address,
Callicoon, Sullivan Co., N. Y.—9 miles from depot. Meets guests if
notified. Stage, 50 cents. Accommodations for 20 ; 8 single rooms ; 2
double rooms ; $5 ; $1 per day. Discount to season guests. Near Post
Office. Mail from New York at 5 P. M. Large farm attached. Streams
so near no guide needed. Furnishes livery—$2 per day for team.

TRAVELER'S HOME C. BAURENFIEND, Proprietor—P. O. Address,
North Branch, Sullivan Co., N. Y.—5 miles from depot. Free transportation. Accommodations for 25 ; 6 single rooms ; 5 double rooms ; $6

single ; $1 to $6 double ; $1 per day. Discount to season guests. In the midst of trout streams and bass and pickerel fishing and hunting grounds. Does not equip sportsmen. Raises vegetables.

MANSION HOUSE—James Sherwood, Proprietor P. O. Address, Jeffersonville, Sullivan Co., N. Y.—11 miles from depot. Stage. Accommodations for 20 ; $5; $1 per day. Trout streams. Good gunning.

JEFFERSONVILLE HOUSE C. Stanton, Proprietor-- P. O. Address, Jeffersonville, Sullivan Co., N. Y.—11 miles from depot. Stage. Accommodations for 20 ; $5; $1 per day.

PIKE POND HOTEL—A. Grouten, Proprietor—P. O. Address, Pike Pond, Sullivan Co., N. Y.—8 miles from depot. Stage. Accommodations for 15 ; $5 ; $1 per day. On the shore of Pike Pond. Bass and pickerel. Free boats for guests.

BOARDING HOUSE.

ALBERT BRANDT—2½ miles from depot. Free transportation. Accommodations for 30 ; 10 single rooms ; 4 double rooms ; $6; $1 per day. Raises vegetables.

FARM HOUSES.

F. WOHLER—P. O. Address, North Branch, Sullivan Co., N. Y.—5 miles from depot. Stage. Accommodations for 40 ; $5 to $7 ; $1 per day.

G. S. GEBHART—P. O. Address, North Branch, Sullivan Co., N. Y. —5 miles from depot. Accommodations for 15 ; $5 to $ 7; $1 per day.

JACOB DIETZ – P. O. Address, Callicoon, Sullivan Co., N. Y.—9 miles from depot. Stage. Accommodations for 15 ; $5 to $7; $1 per day.

E. FISH—P. O. Address, Jeffersonville, Sullivan Co., N. Y.—11 miles from depot. Stage. Accommodations for 18. $5 to $8 ; $1 per day.

R. B. COOPER - P. O. Address, Jeffersonville, Sullivan Co., N. Y.— 11 miles from depot. Stage. Accommodations for 25 ; $5 to $8 ; $1 per day.

PRIVATE HOUSES.

E. FISH, P. O. address, Jeffersonville, Sullivan Co., N. Y.—9 miles from depot. Stage and private conveyance, $1. Accommodations for 18 ; 9 single rooms ; 4 double rooms ; $5 to $8 ; $1 per day. Discount to season guests. Furnishes livery, $2 per day. Pure water. Plenty of shade. House large. Extensive grounds. Raises vegetables.

M. H. ATWATER-- P. O. Address, Callicoon Depot. ¼ mile from depot. Free carriage. Accommodations for 10 ; 5 double rooms ; $4.50 to $6. Raises vegetables.

R. B. COOPER—P. O. Address, Jeffersonville, Sullivan Co., N. Y.— 9 miles from depot. Private conveyance and daily stage, $1. Accommodations for 25 ; 9 single rooms ; 4 double rooms ; $5 to $8 ; $1 per day. Discount to season guests. Croquet lawn, large play-ground. Fine park. Extensive gardens. Fresh fruit, vegetables, eggs, butter, and milk. Furnishes livery, $2 per day.

LIVERY STABLE.

Z. MINARD, MINARD HOUSE—$2 per day for single rig ; $4 for team, with or without driver.

GUIDES.

JNO. B. CONKLIN, O. QUICK, for the Delaware bass fishing. Furnish boats. Z. ROSS, for trout streams, lakes, and hunting grounds—$1.50 per day.

STAGE LINES.

For North Branch (50 cents) and Callicoon (75 cents), Tuesdays, Thursdays, and Saturdays. For Jeffersonville and Pike Pond, daily except Sunday, $1 ; $1.50 round trip. Leave after the arrival train 1 (9.15 A. M. from New York). Connect with train 30 for New York (2:52 P. M.)

------ ◆ • ◆ • ◆ ------

HANCOCK, DELAWARE CO., N. Y.

164 Miles from New York: 4 Trains each way daily; 1 Train from and 3 Trains to New York Sunday.

FARE, $5.

At the junction of the two branches of the Delaware river. Surrounded by mountains. Fifteen trout streams within from one to twelve miles. In the Beaverkill region. Ten lakes near. Deer, bear, partridge. Black bass in the Delaware.

—※—

HOTEL.

HANCOCK HOUSE— E. W. GRIFFIN, Proprietor. Near depot. Accommodations for 25 : 50 single rooms ; 40 double rooms; $5 ; $1 per day. Discount to season party. Livery and farm attached.

IN THE HUDSON HIGHLANDS.

————— ◆ —————

The " Newburgh Short Cut " branch of the Erie, which leaves the main line a mile east of Turner's, opens up a country that is wonderful in many ways. The road runs along the base of the lofty Highlands. The range is cut with deep glens and valleys, and in its rocky crests holds many a shimmering lake. On the left is Schunemunk Mountains. The lake system of the Highlands is one of the greatest marvels of the section. From the Hudson to the New Jersey State line, no less than forty lakes, of different areas and degrees of altitude, and all surpassingly beautiful, nestle among the crags and on the bold plateaus. · Some are still surrounded by the solitude of a century ago. Others occupy charming positions nearer by, and have become noted centres of summer resorts. They are all stocked with bass, pickerel, and other game fish. Over a hundred years ago the waters of some of the lakes were economized for manufacturing purposes, the iron-furnaces of the region being the main industry that they fostered and made successful. As an evidence of the purity of the water comprising them, it may be stated that they are natural trout haunts, and it was not until pickerel and other voracious fish were placed in the lakes that trout disappeared from them.

Aside from the delightful scenery of the Highlands, it is a fact which the experience of years has demonstrated, that the air which circulates among these hills and valleys is possessed of curative properties that render the existence of pulmonary or bronchial difficulties next to an impossibility from the Schunemunk range to the Cornwall Hills. It is stated that there is a well defined line which marks the boundary of this rare mountain atmosphere, and that the area of its presence is within the mountain elevations just mentioned. There are innumerable instances of invalids being restored to robust health by a few seasons spent in the Highlands, prominent among them being the late N. P. Willis, the poet, who visited Cornwall a confirmed consumptive, spent one season in the mountains, and was so much benefited that he became a resident, and was restored to health. The value of this region as a sanitarium is now recognized by leading physicians, and many patients suffering with lung or throat diseases are annually recommended by them to seek some one of the favorite resorts among the Highlands, on the line of the Erie Railway.

They are as follows :

CENTRAL VALLEY, ORANGE CO., N. Y.

49 Miles from New York : 5 Trains from and 6 to New York daily. 1 Train from and 2 to New York Sundays.

Summer Fare—Local, $1.15; Excursion, $2.00; Commutation, 3 Months, $42.75.

HOTEL.

SUMMIT LAKE HOUSE—Elisha Stockbridge, Proprietor—2 miles from depot. Carriage and stage, 50 cents. Accommodations for 80; 12 single rooms; 25 double rooms; $8 to $15 single; $10 double; $1.50 per day. Discount to season guests. In heart of the Highlands. 1,800 feet above tide. 11 mountain lakes. Summit Lake near. Bass and pickerel. Boats and tackle furnished guests; 10 cents per hour; 50 cents per day; boat extra. Woodcock, partridge, fox, rabbit. Hendrix, keeper of Summit Lake, acts as guide to lakes and hunting ground; $1 per day. No charge for dogs. Vegetables, fruits, eggs, milk, chickens, butter, all from the place.

BOARDING HOUSES.

MOTT'S VILLA—E. R. Mott, Proprietor—Five minutes walk from depot. Transportation free. Accommodations for 30; 5 single rooms; 9 double rooms; $8 to $12 single; $30 to $40 double; $2 per day. Handy to the lakes and woods. Raises vegetables.

ISAAC L. NOXSON—¼ mile from depot. Transportation free on arrival of guests and departure at end of season. Accommodations for 60; 7 single rooms; 10 double rooms. First and second floor, 1 in room, $10; 2 in room, $15. Third floor, 1 in room, $7; 2 in room, $11. Same rate for double rooms. Special rates to families. $2.50 from Saturday night till Monday morning. Vegetables, milk, etc., from farm.

MRS. E. GIBB—¼ mile from depot. Free transportation. Accommodations for 40. $8. No discount. Raises vegetables.

DAVID CORNELL—¼ mile from depot. Accommodations for 30; 12 rooms, single and double. $5 to $8; $1 per day. Near lakes. Vegetables, milk, eggs, and butter from the place.

FARM HOUSE.

HENRY THORNE, Sr. —¼ mile from depot. Accommodations for 3 or 4 families, or 20 guests; 3 single rooms; 3 double rooms; $6 single; $7 double; 35 cents per meal. Discount to season guests. Raises vegetables.

PRIVATE HOUSE.

COL. A. H. TAYLOR—¼ mile from depot. Free transportation. Accommodations for 15; $12 to $15. First class.

LIVERY.

E. STOCKBRIDGE, Summit Lake House, E. R. MOTT, S. RUMSEY, C. FORD—50 cents per hour, single rig; $1 per hour, team.

31

HIGHLAND MILLS, ORANGE CO., N. Y.

50 Miles from New York : 5 Trains from and 6 to New York daily ; 1 Train from and 2 to New York Sundays.

SUMMER FARE—LOCAL FARE, $1.15 ; EXCURSION, $2.00 ; COMMUTATION 3 MONTHS, $43.25.

HOTELS.

CROMWELL LAKE HOUSE. OLIVER CROMWELL, Proprietor. 1½ miles from station. Stage meets 9 A. M. train from New York on and after May 15 ; all trains on and after June 1 ; any time on notice by wire or mail ; 25 cents. Accommodations for 150; 70 rooms; $8 to $13, as to room and time. Children and servants as to age and room ; $2 to $2.50 per day. 1,200 feet above tide. High ceilings, broad halls, and piazzas. Perfect ventilation and drainage. On shore of lake. Extensive lawns. Stabling, livery, and laundry. Western Union telegraph office. Boating free. No bar. Wines permitted. Highest New York and Brooklyn references.

BOARDING HOUSE.

C. H. TOWNSEND. Short distance from station. Accommodations for 50. Raises vegetables.

◆ ● ◆ ● ◆

WOODBURY, ORANGE CO., N. Y.

51 Miles from New York : 4 Trains from and 3 to New York daily ; 1 Train from and 2 to New York Sundays.

SUMMER FARES—LOCAL, $1.15; EXCURSION, $2; COMMUTATION, 3 MONTHS, $43.75.

BOARDING HOUSE.

W. J. CORNELL—¼ mile from depot. Transportation free. Accommodations for 25 ; 6 single rooms ; 8 large double rooms ; $7 to $8 per week for single room ; $8 to $10 for double ; transient, $2 per day. Pickerel and bass lakes within easy reach. Furnishes tent, tackle, and makes specialty of taking parties fishing, camping, and picnicking. Boats at reasonable rates. Has livery accommodations. Raises vegetables.

MAPLE CENTRE FARM—LEWIS S. JOYCE, Proprietor—¼ mile from depot. Carriage, 20 cents single ; 15 cents each for more than one. Accommodations for 25 ; 2 single rooms ; 11 double rooms ; $7 single ; $7 to $8 double ; $1.50 from Saturday night until Monday morning. A quiet farming neighborhood. A creek runs through the premises. Vegetables, fruits, milk, butter, eggs, fresh from the farm. Within easy reach of all the lakes. Furnishes livery.

L. A. VAN CLEFT—¼ mile from depot. Free transportation. Accommodations for 30 ; 3 single rooms ; 12 double rooms ; $8 to $10 single ; $12 to $16 double ; $2 per day. Discount to season guests. Raises vegetables. Furnishes livery at reasonable prices.

MOUNTAINVILLE, ORANGE CO., N. Y.

55 Miles from New York: 5 Trains from, 6 Trains to
New York daily; Sunday, 1 Train from, 2
Trains to New York.

Summer Fares—Local, $1.15 ; Excursion, $2 ; Commutation,
3 Months, $16.

BOARDING HOUSES.

TITUS HOUSE—Jacob Cocks, Proprietor—¼ mile from depot.
Transportation, 25 cents. Accommodations for 30 ; 2 single rooms ; 13
double rooms ; $8 single ; $5 to $7 to double ; $1.50 per day. Discount
to season guests. Open May 1. Furnishes livery, $5 to $10 per day.
Raises vegetables.

JOHN ORR—Near depot. Accommodations for 30 ; 4 single rooms ;
9 double rooms ; $8 single ; $16 to $20 double. Spring water. Post-
office, telegraph office, and express office near house. Furnishes livery.
Raises vegetables.

STEPHEN BRUNDAGE—¼ mile from depot. Transportation, party, 10 cents ; single, 25 cents. Accommodations for 25 ; 4 single rooms
in cottage ; 9 double rooms ; $6 and $7 ; $1 per day. Farm of 90
acres. Fresh vegetables, fruits, eggs, butter and milk. High ground.

‑‑‑ ◄•••► ‑‑‑

CORNWALL, ORANGE CO., N. Y.

56 Miles from New York : 5 Trains from New York
and 6 to New York daily ; 1 Train from and 2
to New York Sundays.

Summer Fares—Local, $1.15 ; Excursion, $2 ; Commutation, 3
Months, $16.75 ; Book of 50 Tickets, $30, Valid
3 Months, Either Direction.

The fame of this resort is world wide. Not less than five thousand
people annually summer in the Cornwall district, and among the guests
who are now regular annual visitors there are many who came to Cornwall as invalids years ago. The wonderful therapeutic qualities of the
Cornwall air was first made known to the public generally by the poet
Willis, who took up his residence there twenty-five years ago the
beautiful " Idlewild " that he called into existence being still one of the
attractions of the place. Physicians are now sending patients to Cornwall for affections that it was formerly thought could not be benefited
in a climate other than the Bahamas, Bermudas, or the Lake Superior

region. Storm King and Old Cro' Nest, two ancient crags famed in story and song, belong to Cornwall. The hotels and boarding houses of Cornwall are all of a high class. Accommodations for all kinds are equal to any summer resort in the Union. The drives to West Point, to Newburgh, to New Windsor, and the hundreds of shorter mountain drives and walks are unsurpassed.

—⚹—

HOTELS.

ELMER HOUSE—Wм. B. Elmer, Manager—P. O. address, Cornwall. on-the-Hudson. 1 mile from station. Free transportation. Accommodations for 150 ; 25 single rooms ; 60 double rooms—$2.50 per day. Discount to season guests. 250 feet above Hudson. Fine view of river and mountains. Ground slopes to the water's edge. Spring beds. Large airy rooms. Large garden and grounds. House highly recommended by guests.

C. H. SMITH—3 miles from station. Stage or carriage, 25 cents. Accommodations for 200 ; $10 single ; $16 double ; $2 per day. Discount to season guests. Raises vegetables and fruit.

BOARDING HOUSES.

LINDEN PARK HOUSE—R. B. Ring, Proprietor—1½ miles from depot. Stage 25 cents. Accommodations for 100 ; 50 rooms—$8 to $12 ; $2 per day. Discount to season guests. Everything first-class. Raises fruit and vegetables.

MOODNA MANSION—Wм. Orr, Proprietor—1-3 mile from depot. Stage and private carriage, 10 cents. Accommodations for 50 ; 20 rooms in house ; 8 in cottage attached ; $10 to $12 single ; $12 to $18 double. Has cottage near ; 500 feet above Hudson. Will rent furnished, or let to boarders. Double rooms, $12 ; single, $7. Livery in connection with house. Raises vegetables.

L. P. CLARK · 2½ miles from depot. Stage from all trains, 25 cents. Accommodations for 40 ; 10 single rooms ; 14 double rooms ; $6 to $10 single ; $8 to $12 double ; $2 per day. Discount to season guests. Open winter and summer. House on west bank Hudson, near mouth Moodna Creek ; faces east ; most of the rooms afford view of river. Forest trees. Raises fruit and vegetables.

LAWRENCE HOUSE—J. J. Lawrence, Proprietor—3 miles from depot. Stage 25 cents. Accommodations for 60 ; 20 double rooms— $12 to $18 single ; $18 to $25 double—$2 per day. Discount to season guests. Raises fruit and vegetables.

GLEN RIDGE HOUSE—James G. Roe, Proprietor—3 miles from depot. Carriage and stage, 25 to 50 cents. Accommodations for 250 ; 20 single rooms ; 84 double rooms : $10 to $14 single ; $20, $24, $28 double ; $2 per day. Discount to season guests. Livery on the premises. Gas and water throughout. Spring beds, hair mattresses. Wood fires in rooms if called for. Forty acres adjoining "Idlewild." Glens, shaded walks. Fresh fruit and vegetables a specialty.

BROOKSIDE COTTAGE—Geo. W. Roome, Proprietor—3 miles from station. Stage, 25 cents. Accommodations for 30; 4 single rooms; 16 double rooms; $8 to $10 single; $16 to $20 double; $1.50 per day. Discount to season guests. Raises fruit and vegetables.

VINEBROOK COTTAGE—C. E. Cocks, Proprietor—3½ miles from station. Stage, 25 cents. Accommodations for 25; 11 rooms; $7 for one adult; $12 to $14 for two; $1.25 per day. Discount to season guests. Five minutes from post office, telegraph office, and reading room. Farm of 11 acres. Adjoins farm of E. P. Roe, the author and fruit cultivator. Plenty of fresh fruit. Vegetables, eggs, and milk a specialty.

C. BIRDSALL—3 miles from station. Stage, 25 cents. Accommodations for 50; 8 single rooms; 25 double rooms: $12 single: $24 double; $2 per day. 200 feet above Hudson. Extensive view of Newburgh Bay and the mountain scenery. Good bathing. Raises fruit and vegetables.

T. M. WILEY—2½ miles from depot. Accommodations for 40; 6 single rooms; 25 double rooms—$8 to $10 single; $18 to $20 double— $1.50 per day. Near telegraph office, post office, and reading room. Raises and buys vegetables.

WILLARD AVENUE HOUSE—Mrs. J. O'Brien, Proprietor—2½ miles from depot. Accommodations for 60; 12 single rooms; 10 double rooms, three windows in each; $10 single; $20 double; $1.50 per day; $8 family for season; children $4; nurses $6. Guests have principally been first-class German families. Refers to Mr. A. Hoffman, 100 Gold st., N. Y.; Mr. Geo. Frank, 3 Hanover st., N. Y. Plenty of shade. All kinds of fruit on the place. Large grounds. Claims it as the coolest location in Cornwall.

LIVERY STABLES.

J. William Chatfield, John Chatfield, William Edwards, Wood Bros., and D. T. Hill. Teams, $1.50 for first hour; $1 per hour for each additional hour—$5 to $8 per day; single rigs in the same proportion.

———•◆•◆•———

NEWBURGH, ORANGE CO., N. Y.

63 Miles from New York: 5 Trains from New York and 6 Trains to New York daily; 1 Train from and 2 trains to New York Sundays.

Summer Fares—Local, $1.20; Excursion, $2.25; Commutation, 3 Months, $50; Book of 50 Tickets, $32.50. Valid for 3 Months, Either Direction.

Population, 20,000. On Newburgh Bay. First settled in 1719. One of the shire towns of Orange county. Celebrated for its Revolutionary associations, beautiful scenery, and healthfulness. Washington's Head-quarters in 1782-3. Famous building occupied by him, erected in

1752, still standing. Filled with relics of the Revolution. Points of interest innumerable. Unsurpassed boating and fishing in the Bay. Orange Lake, 6 miles distant; bass and pickerel. Fine drives to Cornwall, West Point, and all places in Highlands. Churches of all denominations. Hotels and boarding houses all first-class.

—⟨⟩—

HOTEL.

UNITED STATES HOTEL. J. C. Griggs, Proprietor—Five minutes walk from depot. Baggage transported free. Accommodations for 125 ; 40 single rooms; 40 double rooms. $8 to $12 single ; $20 to $26 double ; $2.50 per day. Special rates to season guests. Livery attached.

BOARDING HOUSES.

H. W. MURTFELT—3 miles from depot. Carriage transportation, 50 cents. Accommodations for 35 ; 3 single rooms ; 14 double rooms ; $8 single ; $14 to $16 double ; $2 per day. On the banks of the Hudson. Fine drives and walks. Raises fruit and vegetables. P. O. Box 109.

BALDWIN HOUSE—1-3 mile from depot. Free omnibus. Accommodations for 125 ; 23 single rooms ; 33 double rooms ; $7 to $10 single; $10 to $15 double. Discount to season guests. Ten minutes walk from Washington's Headquarters. Building brick. All modern improvements. History of Newburgh and Headquarters sent on application. All vegetables from hotel premises.

LAKE SIDE HOUSE—A. KIDD, Proprietor—6 miles from depot. Stage 50 cents. Accommodations for 70 ; 8 single rooms ; 25 double rooms ; $12 single ; $16 to $20 double ; $2 per day. Discount to season guests. On shore of Orange Lake. Large grounds, plenty of shade. Pickerel, black bass, and perch fishing. Boats free to guests. 1,000 feet above tide. Laundry. Raises vegetables.

HIGHLAND MEDICAL INSTITUTE—DR. J. MITCHEL, Proprietor— 1 mile from depot. Hacks and stages. Accommodations for 30 ; 4 single rooms ; 13 double rooms ; $10 single ; $15 to $20 double ; $2 per day. No discount from June 1 to October 1, except for children and nurses. Telephone connected with livery stables, railroad, telegraph office, and all parts of the city. Highest elevation in city. Unsurpassed views of Hudson Valley, including wonderful entrance to the Highlands. A home for those seeking health or pleasure, or both.

THE LACKAWAXEN VALLEY.

Via Honesdale Branch from Lackawaxen.

ROWLAND'S, PIKE CO., PA.

115 miles from New York ; 2 Trains each way daily,
except Sunday.

FARE, $3.55.

Near Big and Little Tink and Corilla Lakes, and numerous trout
streams. In the hunting region. On the Lackawaxen river.

PRIVATE HOUSE.

G. H. ROWLAND – Short distance from station. Accommodations
for 8 ; 2 single rooms ; 3 double rooms ; all large, airy, and finely furnished ; $10 single ; $8 double ; $1.75 per day. Discount to season
guests. House on high ground. Plenty of fresh vegetables, milk, eggs
and butter. Furnishes livery, $2 to $5 per day. Guides, $1.50 per day.

MILLVILLE, PIKE CO., PA.

119 Miles from New York : 2 Trains each way daily
except Sundays.

FARE, $3.70: EXCURSION (5 DAYS), $5.50.

A romantic spot in the mountains, on the banks of the Lackawaxen
River and Blooming Grove Creek. The centre of a noted hunting and
fishing region. The trout streams of upper Pike county are in easy distance. The Blooming Grove Creek is one of the best of these. Tink,
Big and Little Corilla. Knob, White Deer, and Jones's Lakes are in a
radius of seven miles. Several beautiful waterfalls near. Millville is
the station from which Blooming Grove Park, the famous game preserve of 12,000 acres, is reached by an excellent road, made by the Park
Association. Distance 7 miles. This park has a membership of 50
wealthy and prominent citizens of New York and other cities. A fine
club house, built on the shores of Lake Giles, one of the handsomest
sheets of water in the State, is the property of the Association.

HOTELS.

DEMING HOUSE– JOHN DEMING, Proprietor—Three minutes walk
from depot. Accommodations for 24 ; $7 to $10. Good livery and stabling. Moderate terms. The improvements and facilities that have
made Millville an attractive stopping-place for the summer guest are due
to the efforts of the proprietor of this house.

40

WESTBROOK HOUSE—M. C. WESTBROOK, Proprietor—P. O. Address, Blooming Grove, Pike Co., Pa. Nine miles from depot. Transportation, parties, $1 each ; single passenger, $2. Baggage extra. Accommodations for 15 ; $6 to $10 ; $1.25 per day. In the midst of the Blooming Grove hunting and fishing region. Grand mountain scenery. One mile from Blooming Grove Park. High Knob, loftiest elevation in Northern Pennsylvania, 2,000 feet above tide, 3 miles. Three lakes on the summit of this mountain. Black bass, trout and pickerel fishing unsurpassed. The greatest deer and bear region in the State. Partridge and woodcock. Guides furnished, $1 per day. Guns, dogs, and fishing-tackle. Livery attached. Large farm and dairy. Will also meet guests at Hawley.

BLOOMING GROVE PARK CLUB HOUSE—Eight miles from depot. On shores of Lake Giles. Carriage. Accommodations for 100. Terms arranged on application. 12,000 acres of forest, mountain, lake and stream. Deer, bear and all small game in the preserve. Eight large lakes, stocked with bass, pickerel and perch. A score of trout streams. A retreat for gentlemen sportsmen and their families.

———◆•◆•◆———

HAWLEY, WAYNE CO., PA.

125 Miles from New York : 2 Trains each way daily, except Sundays.

FARE, $3.90 ; EXCURSION (5 DAYS), $5.75.

In the Pike County game and fish region. Trout, bass, and pickerel ; deer, bear, fox, partridge, rabbits. The wonderful Wallenpaupack Falls in the village. Splendid drives. Terminus of the famous Gravity Railroad of the Pennsylvania Coal Company. One of the grandest excursion routes in America. Scranton, 35 miles, heart of Lackawanna coal region. Lake Jones, 6 miles ; White Deer Lake, 9 miles ; Trout streams, from 1 to 8 miles.

——※——

HOTELS.

KEYSTONE HOUSE—WM. SCHARDT, Proprietor—1 minute's walk from West Hawley depot. Accommodations for 40 : 21 single rooms ; 8 double rooms; $8; $1.75 per day. Discount to season guests. Fine location. Near Post office. Furnish livery. Raises vegetables. Guides to streams and hunting grounds. $1.50 per day. Leave cars at upper depot.

EDDY HOUSE—F. MEISINGER, Proprietor—2 minutes walk from depot. Accommodations for 6 single boarders, or 2 small families. $6; $1 per day. On Lackawaxen river. Boats furnished. 10 minutes from Wallenpaupock Falls.

WAYNE COUNTY HOTEL—HERMAN FRANK, Proprietor—10 minutes from depot. Accommodations for 10; $9; $1.50 per day; $32 per month. Owns a lodge at Blooming Grove for special use of sportsmen. Conveyance.

GUIDES.

R. HUFF & BROTHER, ED. QUICK, LAFAYETTE QUICK, LEVI PELTON—$2 per day.

HONESDALE, WAYNE CO., PA.

135 Miles from New York : 2 Trains each way daily, except Sundays.

FARE, $4.40 ; EXCURSION (5 DAYS), $6.75.

One of the handsomest and wealthiest villages in Pennsylvania. Head of the Delaware and Hudson Canal. Lackawaxen and Dyberry rivers run through the place. Streets broad and bordered with maples and elms fifty years old. County seat of Wayne County. Excellent drives. Bethany, 3 miles ; Mart Kimble's, 2 miles ; White Mills, 5 miles ; Waymart, 10 miles. Beautiful park of maples in centre of village. Episcopal, Presbyterian, Methodist, Baptist, Lutheran, and Catholic churches. Twelve famous bass and pickerel lakes within from six to fourteen miles. Trout fishing within from two to five miles. Hotels all first class. Livery unsurpassed. Terminus of the celebrated Gravity Railroad owned by the Delaware and Hudson Canal Company. This road extends to Carbondale, 17 miles, in the upper Lackawanna coal regions. In connection with the similar road from Hawley, it is now one of the most popular excursion routes in America. The cars run up and down high hills, there being no motive power perceptible to the tourist. At one point, an elevation of 2,000 feet above tide is reached. The road curves abruptly around mountains, and traverses glens and the sides of lofty hills. The ride is exhilarating, grand, indescribable. Hundreds of tourists enjoy it daily during the summer and fall months.

—※—

HOTELS.

ALLEN HOUSE—M. B. ALLEN, Proprietor—1 mile from depot. Omnibus, 25 cents ; or will meet guests, if notified. Accommodations for 50; fine large and airy double and single rooms; $6 to $10, single; $10 to $20, double. Special arrangement with season guests. Overlooks park. Splendid location. Broad halls, balconies. Commodious stables. Bath. Vegetables from farm. Free transportation to and from Gravity depots.

KIMBLE HOUSE - M. KIMBLE, Proprietor -2 miles from depot. Meets guests at depot with private conveyance. Accommodations for 10; $5 to $6; $2 per day. Beautiful location. Large farm attached. Surrounded by large shade trees. Rifle range. Croquet lawn. Driving Park ; half-mile track. Commodious stables. All equipments for sportsmen. Plenty of fresh vegetables, fruit, eggs, butter, and milk on the place.

KIPLE HOUSE—R. W. KIPLE, Proprietor—1 mile from depot. Free transportation if notified. Accommodations for 80 : 25 single rooms ; 25 double rooms ; $7 single ; $10 double ; $2 per day. Discount to season guests. Near Post Office and Gravity Railroad. Rooms large and airy. Guides to lakes will be procured.

LIVERY STABLES.

H. T. & G. H. WHITNEY, WHITNEY & KEENE, ENSIGN EGLESTON.— $3 to $5 per day.

ON THE NEWBURGH BRANCH.

West of the Schunemunk Mountains is the romantic valley of the Murderer's Kill, through which the branch of the Erie Railway extending from Greycourt to Newburgh passes. The valley, like this entire section of Orange County, is full of historical associations. The Newburgh Branch and the Short Cut unite at Vail's Gate, six miles from Newburgh. It was at the former place that Generals St. Clair and Gates were quartered when the army was encamped in the vicinity. The Edmoston House, their headquarters, is still standing. It was built in 1755. At Washington Square, two miles from Vail's Gate, General Clinton had his headquarters in the Falls House, still intact. An ancient Indian burying-ground, and a number of very old churches are in the vicinity. Pickerel, bass, and perch fishing in the adjacent lakes. The sojourning places along this Branch that have become very popular among people who love true pastoral surroundings, are as follows:

WASHINGTONVILLE, ORANGE CO., N. Y.

61 Miles from New York: 2 Trains from and 3 to New York daily ; 1 Train each way Sundays.

FARE—LOCAL, $1.85 ; EXCURSION, $2.50 ; COMMUTATION, 3 MOS. $50.50.

BOARDING HOUSES.

MISS A. E. BROOKS—Five minutes walk from depot. Accommodations for 20; $6 to $8. $1.50 per day. Raises vegetables.

T. B. CAMERON—¼ mile from depot. Accommodations for 20 : 4 single rooms ; 5 very large double rooms ; $6 single ; $8 double ; $1.50 per day. Has a horse and carriage. Vegetables and fruit raised on place and in vicinity.

FARM HOUSES.

MISS M. BEATTY—3 miles from depot. Transportation free. Accommodations for 10 ; 1 single room, 7 double rooms; $6 single, $5 to $8 double, according to number. Discount to season guests. Broad piazzas. Extensive grounds. Plenty of shade. Vegetables, fruits, eggs, butter and milk from the farm. Furnishes livery.

DANIEL T. MEAD—1¾ miles from depot. Accommodations for 12; 2 single rooms ; 4 double rooms ; $5 single ; $14 double. House large and cool. Stream runs through premises. Maple grove. Fresh vegetables, milk, eggs, and butter.

LIVERY.

CAMERON, McCANN, MOORE—$2 to $3 per day, single rigs. Team, $5.

SALISBURY, ORANGE CO., N. Y.

63 1-2 Miles from New York: 3 Trains from and 3 to New York daily; 1 Train each way Sundays.

FARE—LOCAL, $1.95; EXCURSION, $2.60; COMMUTATION, 3 MOS., $52.

WOANGDALE VILLA—R. WALLACE GENUNG, Proprietor—2½ miles from depot. Free transportation. Accommodations for 14; 7 double rooms; $8 per week; $1.50 per day. Discount to season guests. Unusually healthful. Grand view for 20 miles. Near the old Governor Clinton homestead. One mile from Highlands. - Fresh vegetables, fruit, eggs, milk and butter from the farm.

———◂●◆●▸———

WARWICK, ORANGE CO., N. Y.

64 Miles from New York, via Erie Railway to Greycourt; thence via Warwick Valley Railroad.

FARE—LOCAL, $2; EXCURSION, $2.75; COMMUTATION, 3 MOS., $56.25.

Warwick and region around it furnishes great attraction to the tourist. Settled in 1720. Sugar-Loaf Mountain, Sterling Mountain, Mount Adam and Mount Eve, are notable features of the landscape. The Drowned Lands, covering 17,000 acres of this part of Orange County, and 2,500 of Sussex County, N. J., are near. Old Sterling iron-furnace, near the outlet of Sterling Lake. Founded by Lord Sterling in 1751. Partridge, quail, woodcock, pickerel, and black bass. Greenwood Lake, 6½ miles; Glenmere, 4½ miles; Wawayanda Lake, 7½ miles; Double Lake, 5 miles; Wickham's Lake, 3 miles. Tackle provided at them all. Warwick Woodlands near.

———✳———

BOARDING HOUSES.

WM. L. BENEDICT—¾ mile from depot. Free transportation. Accommodations for 20; 9 single rooms; 2 double rooms; $6 to $8 single; double, according to number in family. Large and convenient farm house. Spacious grounds, well shaded. Especially adapted, to comfort of families with children. Sportsmen have use of blooded bird-dog. Surroundings cheerful, healthful and attractive. Abundance of vegetables, fruit, milk, eggs and butter, fresh from the farm. Highly recommended.

MRS. ROY—¼ mile from Stonebridge depot, 1½ mile from Warwick. Transportation 50c. Accommodations for 8; rooms large; $6 per week; transient, $1 per day; 5 miles from Greenwood Lake. Fine drive. Excellent locality for children. Raises vegetables. "Not style, but comfort." P. O. address, Warwick, Orange Co., N. Y.

MRS. C. B. VAN DEVORT—Short walk from depot. Accommodations for 11; 3 single rooms; 3 double rooms; $8 single; $7 double; $1.50 per day. Discount to season guests. Raises vegetables.

FARM HOUSE.

KILCARE COTTAGE –A. M. Hoyt, Proprietor–3 miles from depot. Free carriage. Accommodations for 20; 1 single room; 11 double rooms; $7 single; $14 double. No discount. Woods and mountains; 9 miles from Greenwood Lake; 4 miles from Wawayanda Lake. Fresh farm products daily.

LIVERY.

T. E. DEMAREST, N. DUNHAM, N. BAIRD--Good accommodations. $3 to $5 per day.

GUIDES.

EMBLER & BRADNER—Charge according to number in party.

— ◆◆◆◆ —

IN THE CATSKILLS.

— ◆ —

Via Erie Railway to Goshen, thence via Montgomery Branch and Walkill Valley Railroad to Kingston, thence via Ulster and Delaware Railroad.

———

OLIVE BRANCH, ULSTER CO., N. Y.

12 Miles from Kingston.

BOARDING HOUSE.

ALBERT ELMENDORF - P. O. address, Olive, Ulster Co., N. Y. Two miles from depot. Free transportation on notice. Accommodations for 25; 11 single rooms; $5 to $8; $1 per day; discount to season guests. Fishing in Temple Pond. Trout brook near. Acts as guide. $2 per day.

SHOKAN, ULSTER CO., N. Y.

18 Miles from Kingston.

FARM BOARDING HOUSE.

J. M. BURGHER—1½ miles from depot. P. O. Address, West Shokan, Ulster Co., N. Y. Transportation free for season guests, transient, 50 cents. Accommodations for 20; 4 single rooms; 8 double rooms; $7 single; $11 double. Near Whitenburg, Buchkill, and Rondout Creeks. Trout, woodcock, quail, and partridge.

GUIDE.

M. BURGHER—$1.50 per day.

LIVERY.

C. C. WINNE (Private)—$3 to $5 per day.

———— ◦•◆•► ————

BIG INDIAN, ULSTER CO., N. Y.

36 Miles from Kingston.

BOARDING HOUSE.

SLIDE MOUNTAIN HOUSE—B. DUTCHER, Proprietor—3 miles from depot. Free transportation to season guests. Accommodations for 40; 25 rooms. Apply for terms. Near base of Slide Mountain. Trout fishing in head waters of Neversink and Beaverkill streams. Catskill guides furnished, $2 per day. Trout ponds rear of house for pleasure of ladies. Trout dinners prepared to order.

LOCAL EXCURSION TICKETS.

Extension of Time-Limit Thereon.

Commencing with the month of June, 1881, the New York, Lake Erie and Western Railroad Company will extend the time-limit on Local Excursion Tickets as follows :

For all Stations on the Eastern Division and Branches between and including Port Jervis and Suffern, Excursion Tickets will be valid on day of date and *Two Days* thereafter.

For Pond Eddy and Shohola, on the Delaware Division, Excursion Tickets will be valid on day of date and *Three Days* thereafter.

For Lackawaxen, Narrowsburg, Cochecton and Callicoon, on the Delaware Division, and for stations on the Honesdale Branch, Excursion Tickets will be valid on day of date and *Four Days* thereafter.

This arrangement is made solely for the accommodation of summer visitors and will be in force only during the months of June, July, August and September of *this year*.

☞ Excursion Tickets will be good for continuous passage on passenger trains stopping as per time table at the Stations named on the Tickets, during the time-limit as stated on their face, but will not be honored after the expiration of the time-limit. Except that in the case of Excursion Tickets to or from New York or Jersey City, on which the printed time limit is *five days or less,* if a Sunday or legal Holiday intervenes between the date of purchase and the expiration of the time-limit such Tickets will be valid for as many additional days as there are Sundays or legal Holidays included in the printed time-limit.